AF594054

life of the city

edited by
Sarah Hermanson Meister

new york photographs
from the museum of modern art

Library of Congress Control Number: 2007932323
ISBN: 978-0-87070-720-9

Published by The Museum of Modern Art
11 West 53 Street, New York, NY 10019-5497
www.moma.org
Produced by the Department of Publications
The Museum of Modern Art, New York
Edited by Rebecca Roberts
Text section compiled by Brigid von Preussen
Designed by Amanda Washburn and Gina Rossi
Production by Christina Grillo
Research by Priscilla Fraser, Whitney Gaylord, and Carey Gibbons
Printed and bound by Oceanic Graphic Printing
Printed on 128 gsm NPI Matt Artpaper

Distributed in the United States and Canada by
D.A.P./Distributed Art Publishers, Inc., New York

Distributed outside the United States and Canada by
Thames & Hudson, Ltd., London

Front cover: Berenice Abbott. *New York at Night*. 1932 [see page 60]
Back cover: Dan Weiner. *New Year's Eve, Times Square*. 1951 [see page 21]

64 pages: 66 illustrations

Printed in China

photograph credits

The Museum of Modern Art, New York, Digital Imaging Studio: pp. 9–11, 13 (top, bottom), 14, 15, 17–19 (top), 21–23 (top), 24–26, 29, 32 (top, bottom)–34, 36, 39–41, 44–46 (left, right), 49, 51 (bottom), 52, 54, 57–59 (top), 60, 61; The Museum of Modern Art, New York, Digital Imaging Studio, photograph by Thomas Griesel: pp. 12, 20, 28, 37, 48, 51 (top), 55 (bottom); The Museum of Modern Art, New York, Digital Imaging Studio, photograph by Jonathan Muzikar: pp. 19 (bottom), 23 (bottom), 27, 31, 38, 42, 43 (bottom), 47 (top, bottom), 50 (top), 53, 55 (top), 56, 59 (left, right, bottom); The Museum of Modern Art, New York, Digital Imaging Studio, photograph by John Wronn: pp. 16, 30, 43 (top)

bibliographic information

Woody Allen. From "Examining Psychic Phenomena." In *Without Feathers*. New York: Ballantine, 1986. First published 1972; **G. K. Chesterton.** From "What I Saw in America." In *The Collected Works of G. K. Chesterton*. Fort Collins, Colo.: Ignatius Press, 1990. First published 1922; **Joan Didion.** From "Goodbye to All That." In *Slouching Towards Bethlehem*. New York: Farrar, Straus and Giroux, 1968; **Langston Hughes.** "Projection." In *The Collected Poems of Langston Hughes*, edited by Arnold Rampersad with David Roessel, assoc. ed. New York: Random House, 1994. First published 1951. © 1994 Estate of Langston Hughes. Used by permission of Alfred A. Knopf, a division of Random House, Inc.; **Jane Jacobs.** From *The Death and Life of Great American Cities*. New York: Vintage, 1992. First published 1961; **Joyce Kilmer.** From "Incongruous New York." In *The Circus and Other Essays*. Amsterdam: Fredonia Books, 2003. First published 1916; **Le Corbusier.** From "The Fairy Catastrophe." In *When the Cathedrals Were White*. New York: McGraw-Hill, 1964. First published 1936; **Toni Morrison.** From *Jazz*. New York: Alfred A. Knopf, 1992; **Lewis Mumford.** From *Sketches from Life: The Autobiography of Lewis Mumford*. New York: Dial Press, 1982; **Ogden Nash.** From "I Want New York." In *Verses from 1929 On*. New York: Little, Brown & Company, 1959. First published 1931. © 1930 Ogden Nash; reprinted by permission of Curtis Brown, Ltd.; **Ezra Pound.** From "Patria Mia." In *Selected Prose 1909–1965*, edited by William Cookson. New York: New Directions, 1973. First published 1913; **John Steinbeck.** From "Autobiography: Making of a New Yorker," *New York Times Magazine*, February 1, 1953; **E. B. White.** From *Here is New York*. New York: The Little Bookroom, 2000. First published 1949; **Thomas Wolfe.** From *The Web and the Rock*. Baton Rouge: Louisiana State University Press, 1999. First published 1937

Berenice Abbott's 1939 statement, quoted in the foreword, appears in the introduction to Bonnie Yochelson's book *Changing New York* (New York: New Press, 1999).

foreword

Throughout the twentieth century, artists have been inspired by the grit and dynamism of New York City. The city, which became modern in tandem with photography (and in the same brash, undisciplined way), has been a particularly vital subject for photographers, both those who have visited and those who are here to stay. As these individuals explored New York with their cameras, they simultaneously explored what the art of photography might become. The photographer Berenice Abbott once mused, "How shall the two-dimensional print in black and white suggest the flux of activity of the metropolis, the interaction of human beings and solid architectural constructions, all impinging upon each other in time?" Each of the photographs reproduced here is a unique answer to this question.

The images created through the sustained, lively, and diverse engagement of photographers with New York City have formed a critical part of New Yorkers' sense of their city and of themselves. And, cumulatively, photographs of New York have defined the image of the city in the imagination of the world. The sampling of texts that introduces the photographs in this volume suggests a parallel phenomenon in modern literature.

The Museum of Modern Art's collection extensively represents this deeply symbiotic relationship between photography and the Museum's hometown. This book reproduces sixty-six photographs—made by artists following their own curiosity and by professionals on assignment—forming a chronicle of the life of the city.

—Sarah Hermanson Meister, Associate Curator,
Department of Photography

life of the city

And New York is the most beautiful city in the world?

It is not far from it. No urban nights are like the nights there. I have looked down across the city from high windows. It is then that the great buildings lose reality and take on their magical powers. They are immaterial; that is to say one sees but the lighted windows.

Squares after squares of flame, set and cut into the ether. Here is our poetry, for we have pulled down the stars to our will.

—**Ezra Pound**, 1913

The dwellers in a great European city would give their proudest avenue of great shops and rich clubs some dignified and significant title, like the Rue de la Paix or the Friedrichstrasse. The Asiatics would give it a name more definitely descriptive and laudatory, like "The Street of the Thousand and One Mirrors of Delight." The New Yorkers, "laconic and Olympian," designate it by a simple numeral. They call it Fifth Avenue. . . .

To give a street of wonders an austere name, to build palaces and fill them with offices and shops—these are the acts by which Americans are known. And especially does the New Yorker delight in the whimsical, the inconsistent, the unexpected. He is like a child who likes to dig in the sand with a silver spoon and to eat porridge with a toy shovel.

—**Joyce Kilmer**, 1916

There is a sense in which New York is always new; in the sense that it is always being renewed. A stranger might well say that the chief industry of the citizens consists of destroying their city; but he soon realizes that they always start it all over again with undiminished energy and hope. At first I had a fancy that they never quite finished putting up a big building without feeling that it was time to pull it down again; and that somebody began to dig up the first foundations while somebody else was putting on the last tiles. This fills the whole of this brilliant and bewildering place with a quite unique and unparalleled air of rapid ruin.

—**G. K. Chesterton**, 1922

I Want New York

For New York is a wonder city, a veritable fairyland
With many sights not to be seen in Massachusetts or Maryland.
It is situated on the island of Manhattan
Which I prefer to such islands as Welfare or Staten.
And it is far superior
To the cities of the interior.
What if it has a heterogeneous populace?
That is one of the privileges of being a metropulace
And heterogeneous people don't go around bothering each other
And you can be reasonably sure that everything you do won't get right back
to your dear old mother.

—**Ogden Nash**, 1931

A hundred times I have thought: New York is a catastrophe, and fifty times: it is a beautiful catastrophe.

—**Le Corbusier**, 1936

Now the train was slowing to a halt. Long tongues of cement now appeared, and faces, swarming figures, running forms beside the train. And all these faces, forms, and figures slowed to instancy, were held there in the alertness of expectant movement. There was a grinding screech of brakes, a slight jolt, and, for a moment, utter silence.

At this moment there was a terrific explosion.

It was New York.

—**Thomas Wolfe**, 1937

There are roughly three New Yorks. There is, first, the New York of the man or woman who was born here, who takes the city for granted and accepts its size and its turbulence as natural and inevitable. Second, there is the New York of the commuter—the city that is devoured by locusts each day and spat out each night. Third, there is the New York of the person who was born somewhere else and came to New York in quest of something. Of these three trembling cities the greatest is the last — the city of final destination, the city that is a goal. It is this third city that accounts for New York's high-strung disposition, its poetical deportment, its dedication to the arts, and its incomparable achievements. Commuters give the city its tidal restlessness; natives give it solidity and continuity; but the settlers give it passion.

— **E. B. White**, 1949

Projection

On the day when the Savoy
leaps clean over to Seventh Avenue
and starts jitterbugging
with the Renaissance,
on that day when Abyssinia Baptist Church
throws her enormous arms around
St. James Presbyterian
and 409 Edgecombe
stoops to kiss 12 West 133rd,
on that day—
Do, Jesus!
Manhattan Island will whirl
like a Dizzy Gillespie transcription
played by Inez and Timme.
On that day, Lord,
Willie Bryant and Marian Anderson
will sing a duet,
Paul Robeson
will team up with Jackie Mabley,
and Father Divine will say in truth,
        Peace!
        It's truly
        wonderful!

— **Langston Hughes**, 1951

New York is an ugly city, a dirty city. Its climate is a scandal, its politics are used to frighten children, its traffic is madness, its competition is murderous. But there is one thing about it—once you have lived in New York and it has become your home, no place else is good enough.

—**John Steinbeck**, 1953

A good city street neighborhood achieves a marvel of balance between its people's determination to have essential privacy and their simultaneous wishes for differing degrees of contact, enjoyment or help from the people around. This balance is largely made up of small, sensitively managed details, practiced and accepted so casually that they are normally taken for granted.

Perhaps I can best explain this subtle but all-important balance in terms of the stores where people leave keys for their friends, a common custom in New York. In our family, for example, when a friend wants to use our place while we are away for a weekend or everyone happens to be out during the day, or a visitor for whom we do not wish to wait up is spending the night, we tell such a friend that he can pick up the key at the delicatessen across the street. Joe Cornacchia, who keeps the delicatessen, usually has a dozen or so keys at a time for handing out like this. He has a special drawer for them.

—**Jane Jacobs**, 1961

Quite simply, I was in love with New York. I do not mean "love" in any colloquial way, I mean that I was in love with the city, the way you love the first person who ever touches you and never love anyone quite that way again. I remember walking across Sixty-second Street one twilight that first spring, or the second spring, they were all alike for a while. I was late to meet someone but I stopped at Lexington Avenue and bought a peach and stood on the corner eating it and knew that I had come out of the West and reached the mirage. I could taste the peach and feel the soft air blowing from a subway grating on my legs and I could smell lilac and garbage and expensive perfume and I knew that it would cost something sooner or later—because I did not belong there, did not come from there—but when you are twenty-two or twenty-three, you figure that later you will have a high emotional balance, and be able to pay whatever it costs. I still believed in possibilities then, still had the sense, so peculiar to New York, that something extraordinary would happen any minute, any day, any month.

—**Joan Didion**, 1968

There is no question there is an unseen world. The problem is, how far is it from midtown, and how late is it open?

—**Woody Allen**, 1972

Yes: I loved the great bridges and walked back and forth over them, year after year. But as often happens with repeated experiences, one memory stands out above all others: a twilight hour in early spring—it was March, I think—when, starting from the Brooklyn end, I faced into the west wind sweeping over the rivers from New Jersey. The ragged, slate-blue cumulus clouds that gathered over the horizon left open patches for the light of the waning sun to shine through, and finally, as I reached the middle of the Brooklyn Bridge, the sunlight spread across the sky, forming a halo around the jagged mountain of skyscrapers, with the darkened loft buildings and warehouses huddling below in the foreground.

—**Lewis Mumford**, 1982

I'm crazy about this City.

Daylight slants like a razor cutting the buildings in half. In the top half I see looking faces and it's not easy to tell which are people, which the work of stonemasons. Below is shadow where any blasé thing takes place: clarinets and lovemaking, fists and the voices of sorrowful women. A city like this one makes me dream tall and feel in on things. Hep. It's the bright steel rocking above the shade below that does it. When I look over strips of green grass lining the river, at church steeples and into the cream-and-copper halls of apartment buildings, I'm strong. Alone, yes, but top-notch and indestructable.

—**Toni Morrison**, 1992

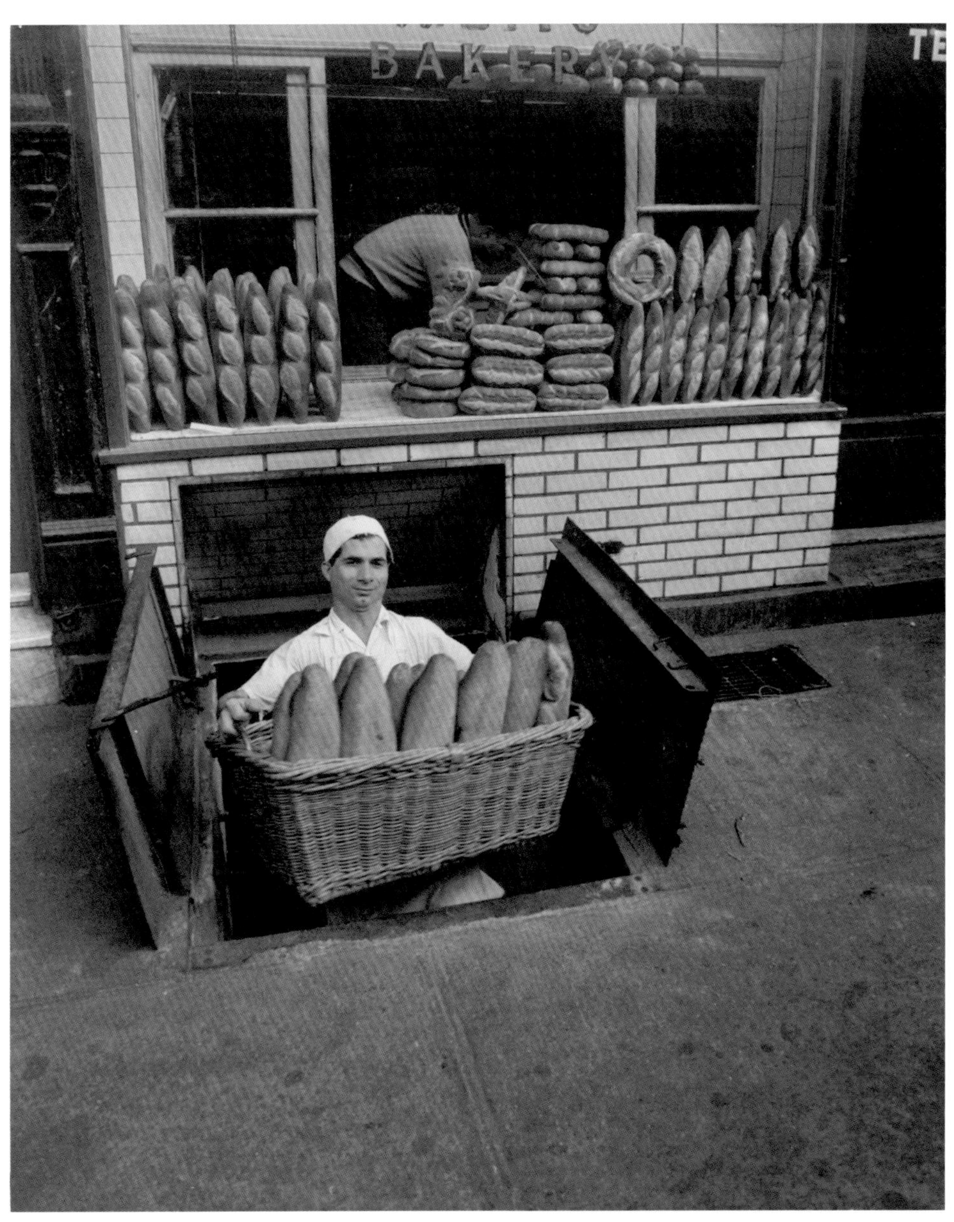

Berenice Abbott. *Zito's Bakery, Bleecker Street*. c. 1948

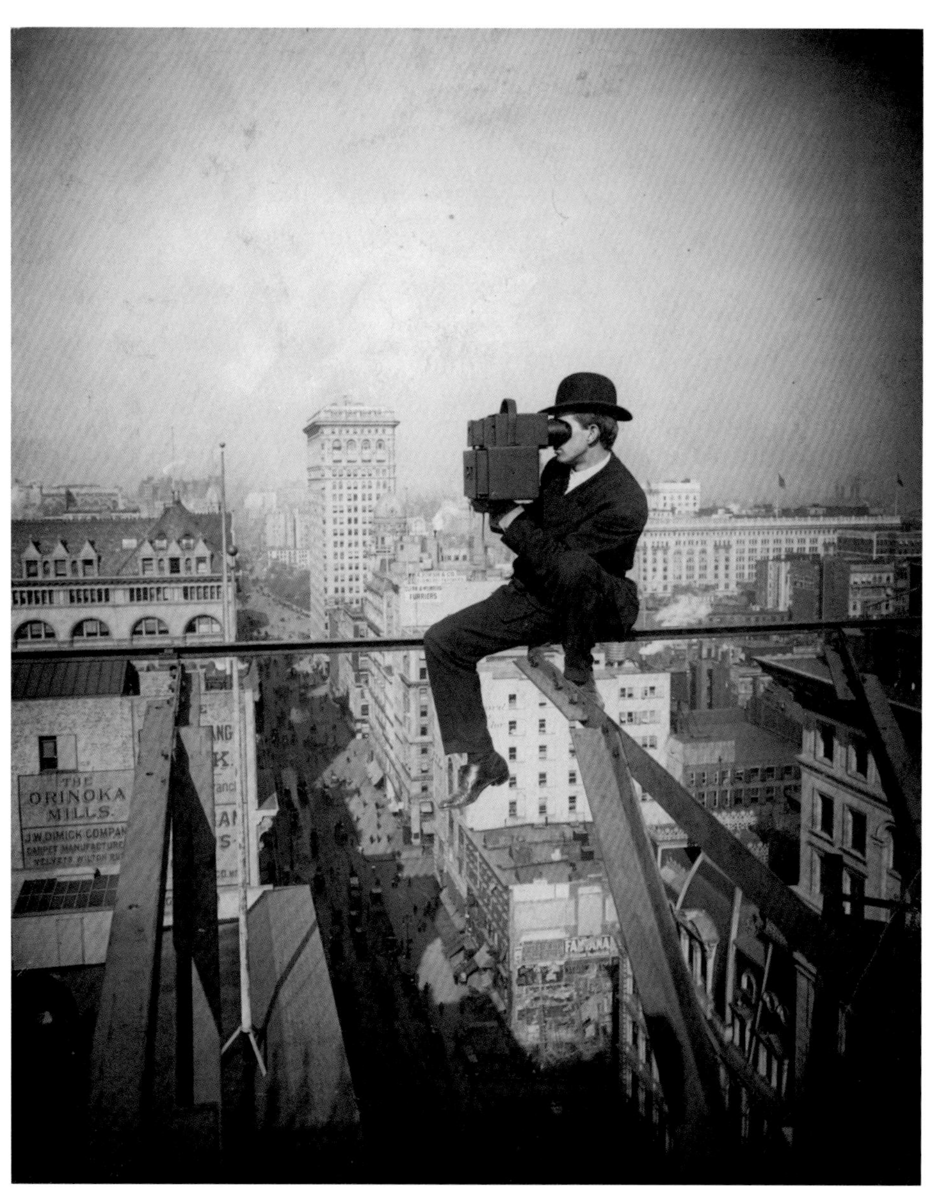

Underwood and Underwood. *Above Fifth Avenue, Looking North*. 1905

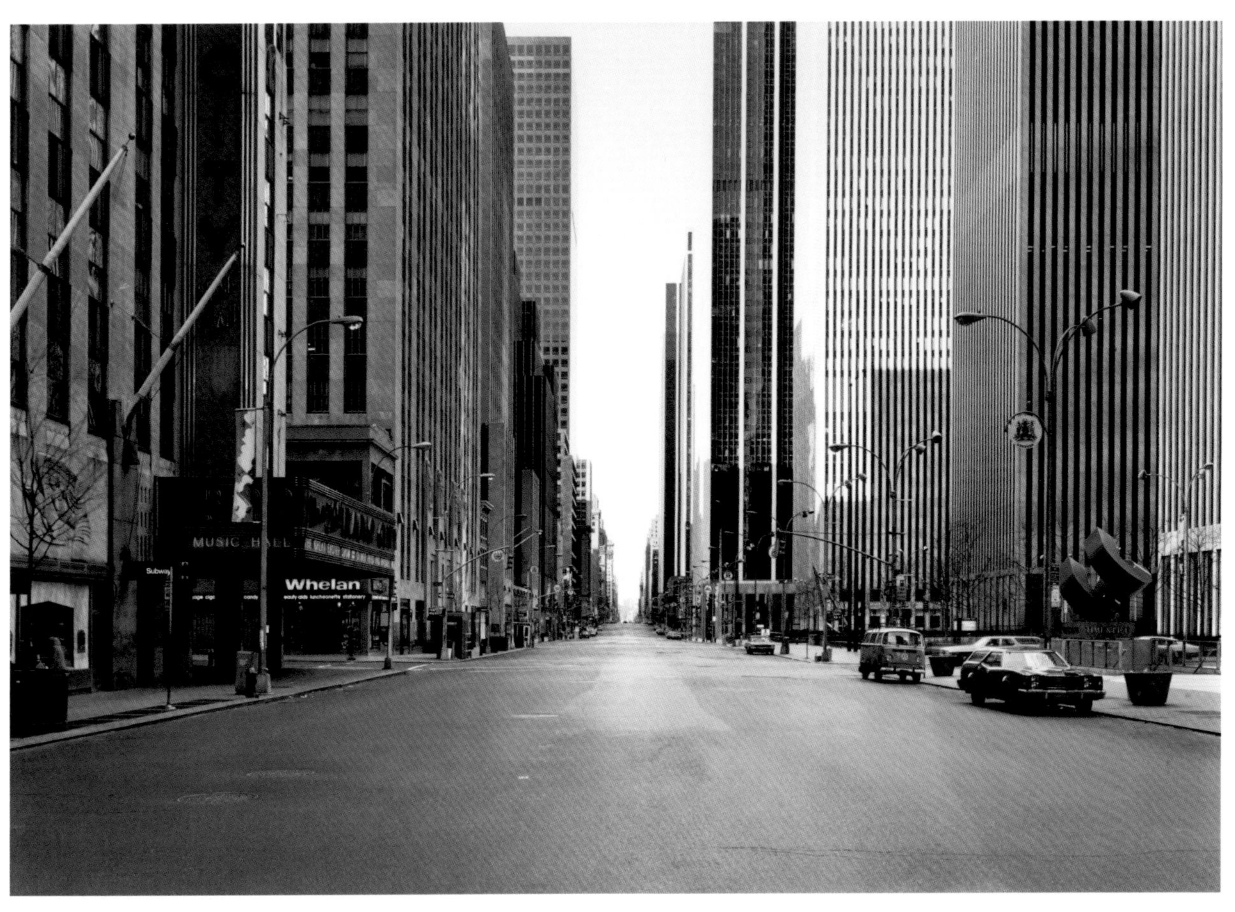

Thomas Struth. *Sixth Avenue at 50th Street, New York/Midtown*. 1978

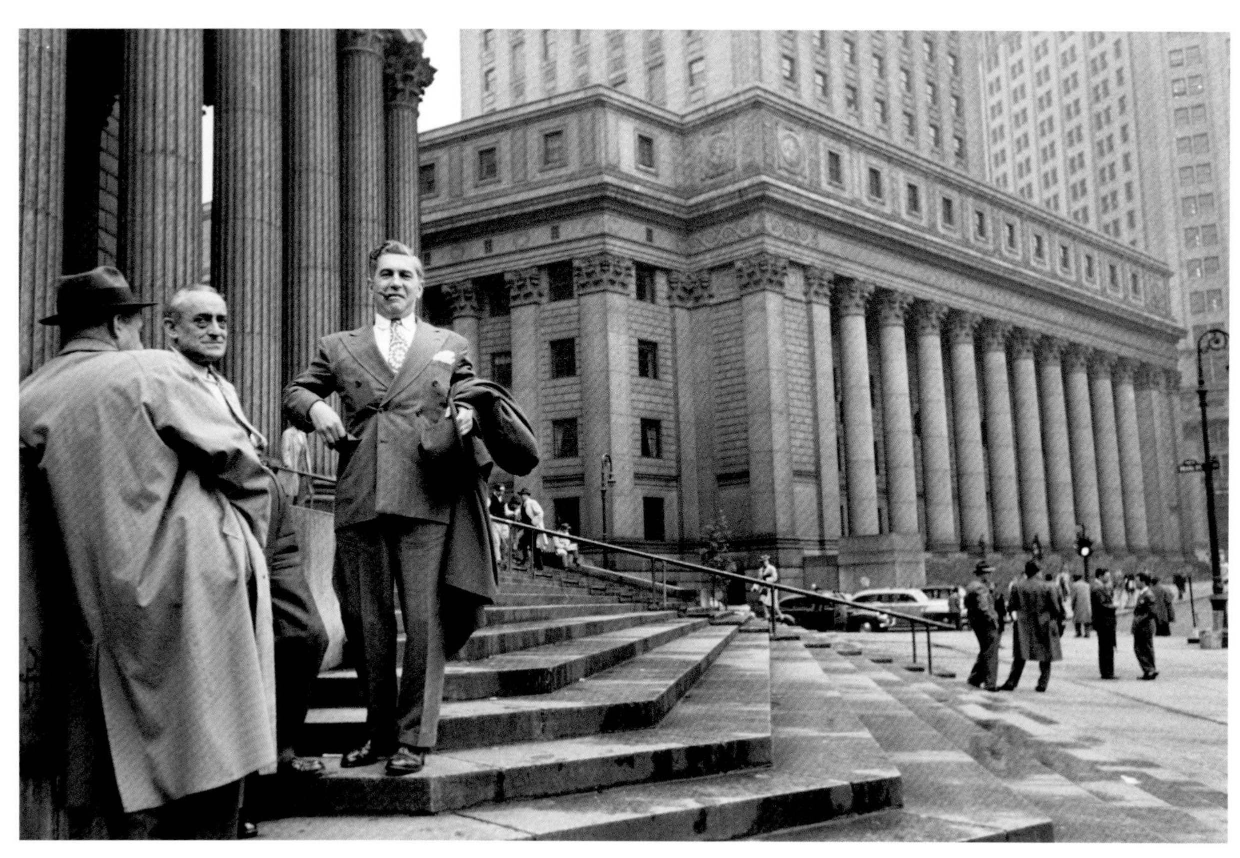

Henri Cartier-Bresson. *Near the Hall of Records, New York*. 1947

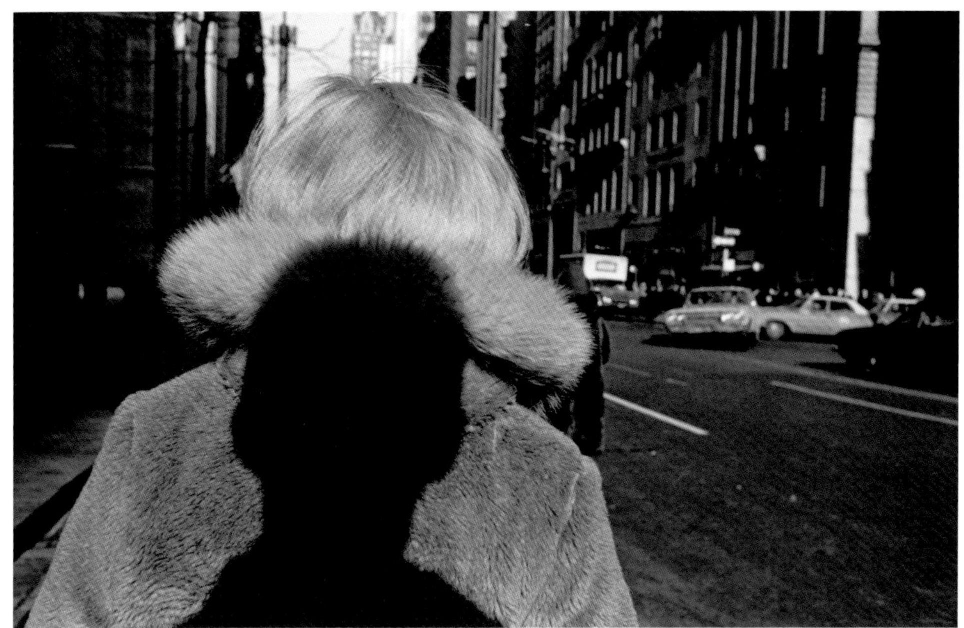

Lee Friedlander. *New York City*. 1966

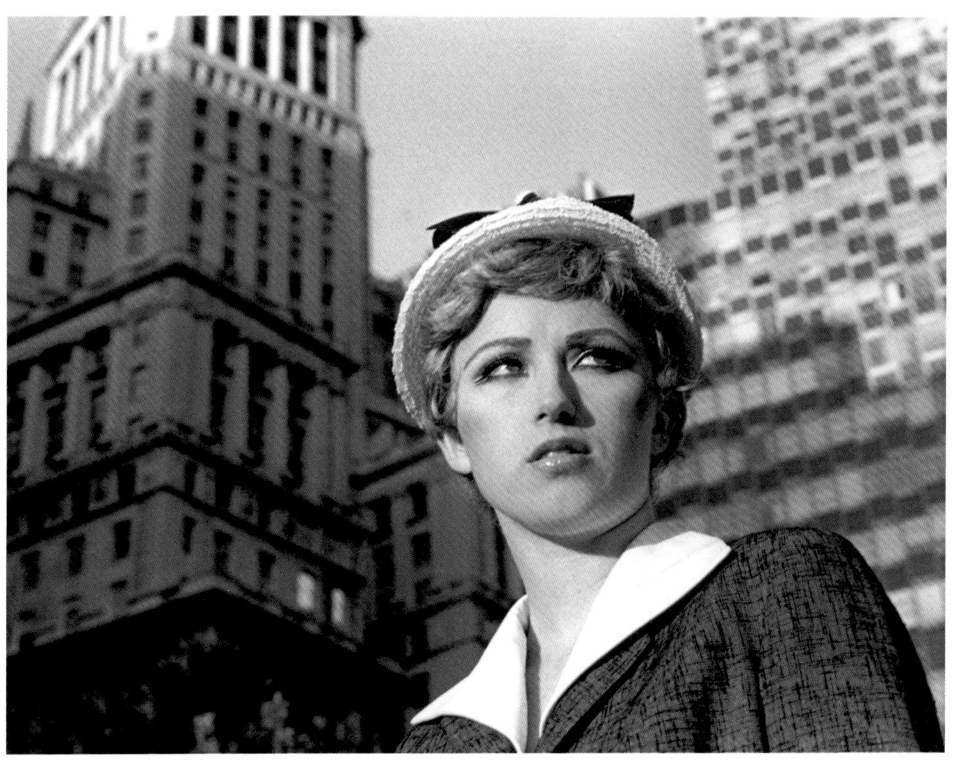

Cindy Sherman. *Untitled Film Still #21*. 1978

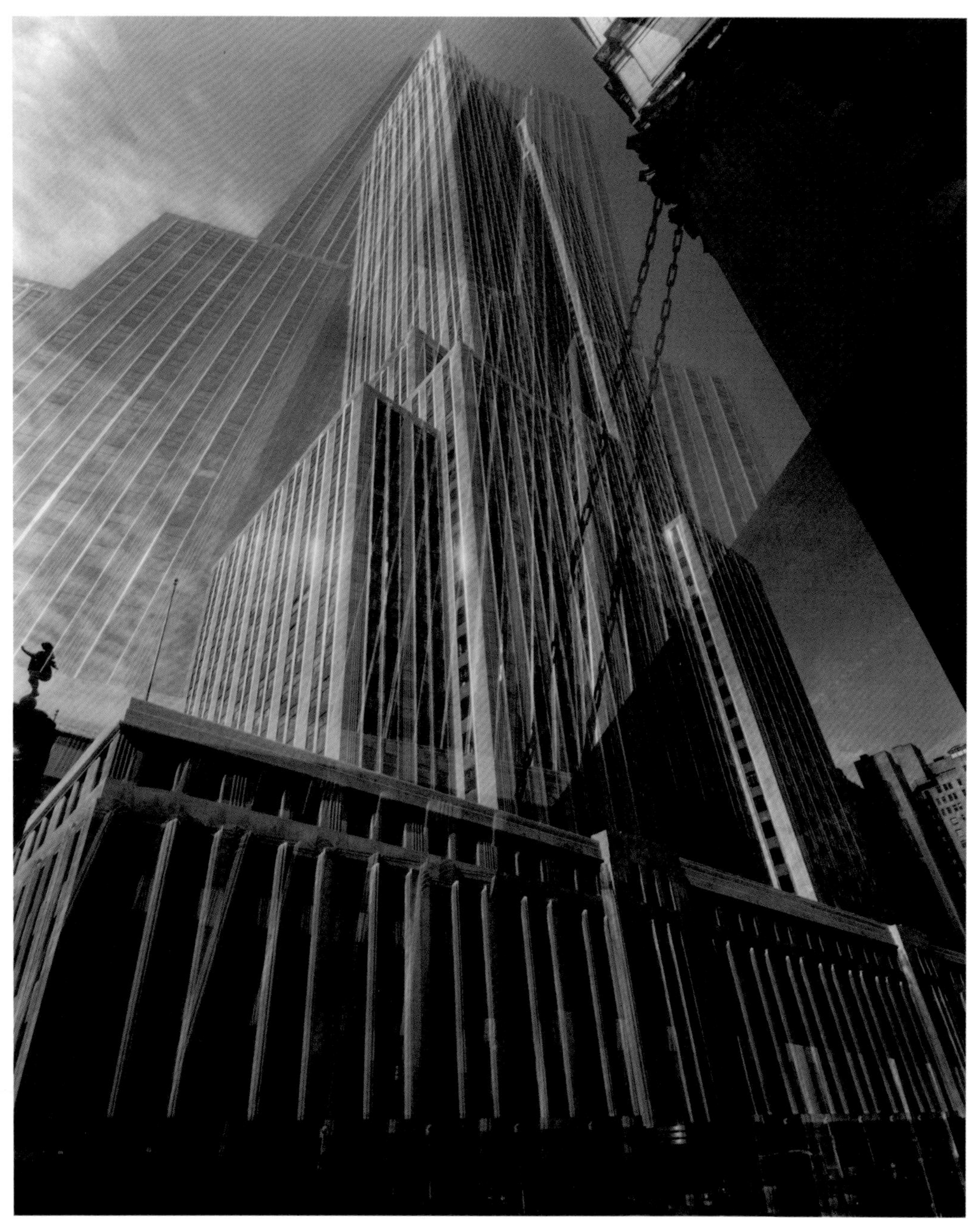

Edward Steichen. *The Maypole*. 1932

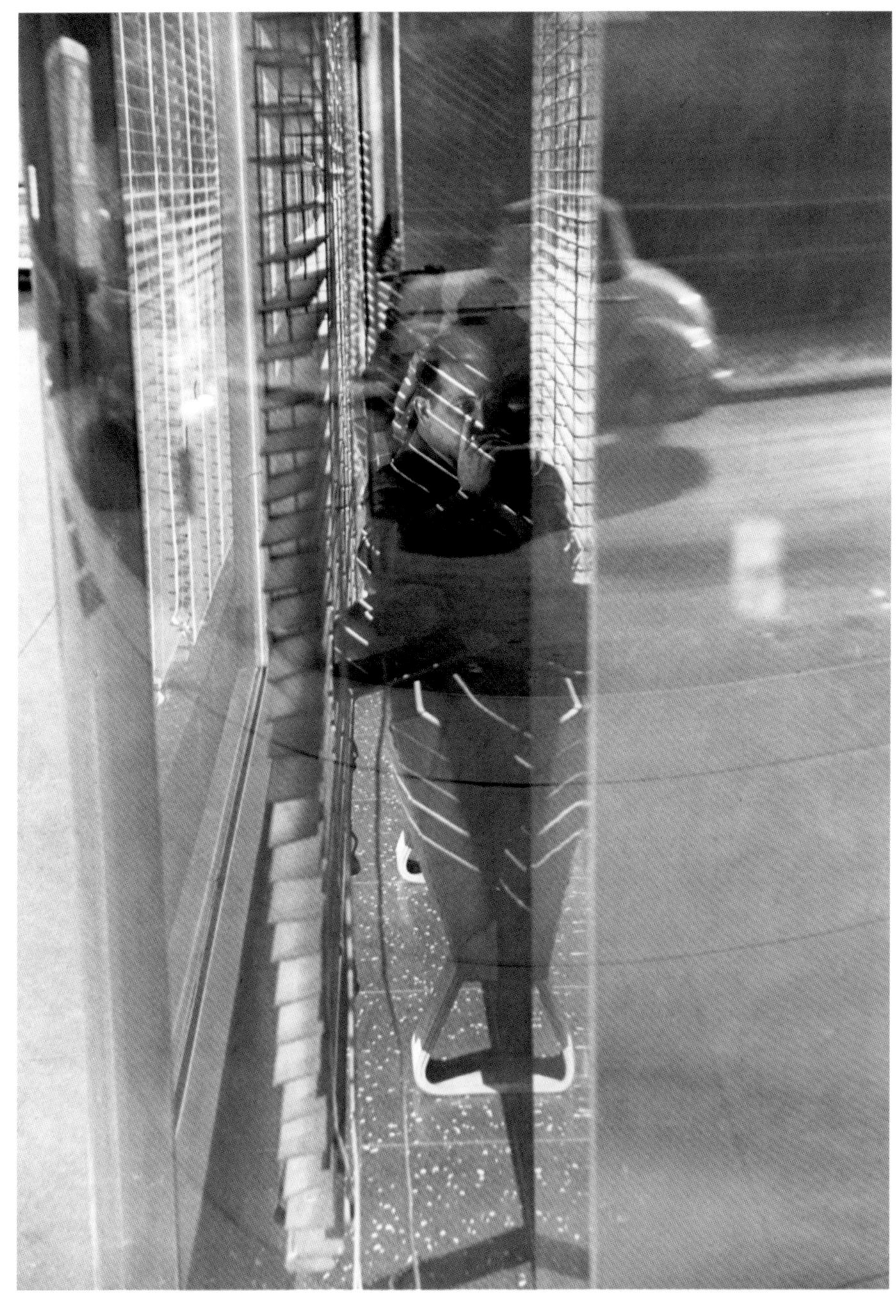

Henri Cartier-Bresson. *An Eye at The Museum of Modern Art, New York*. 1947

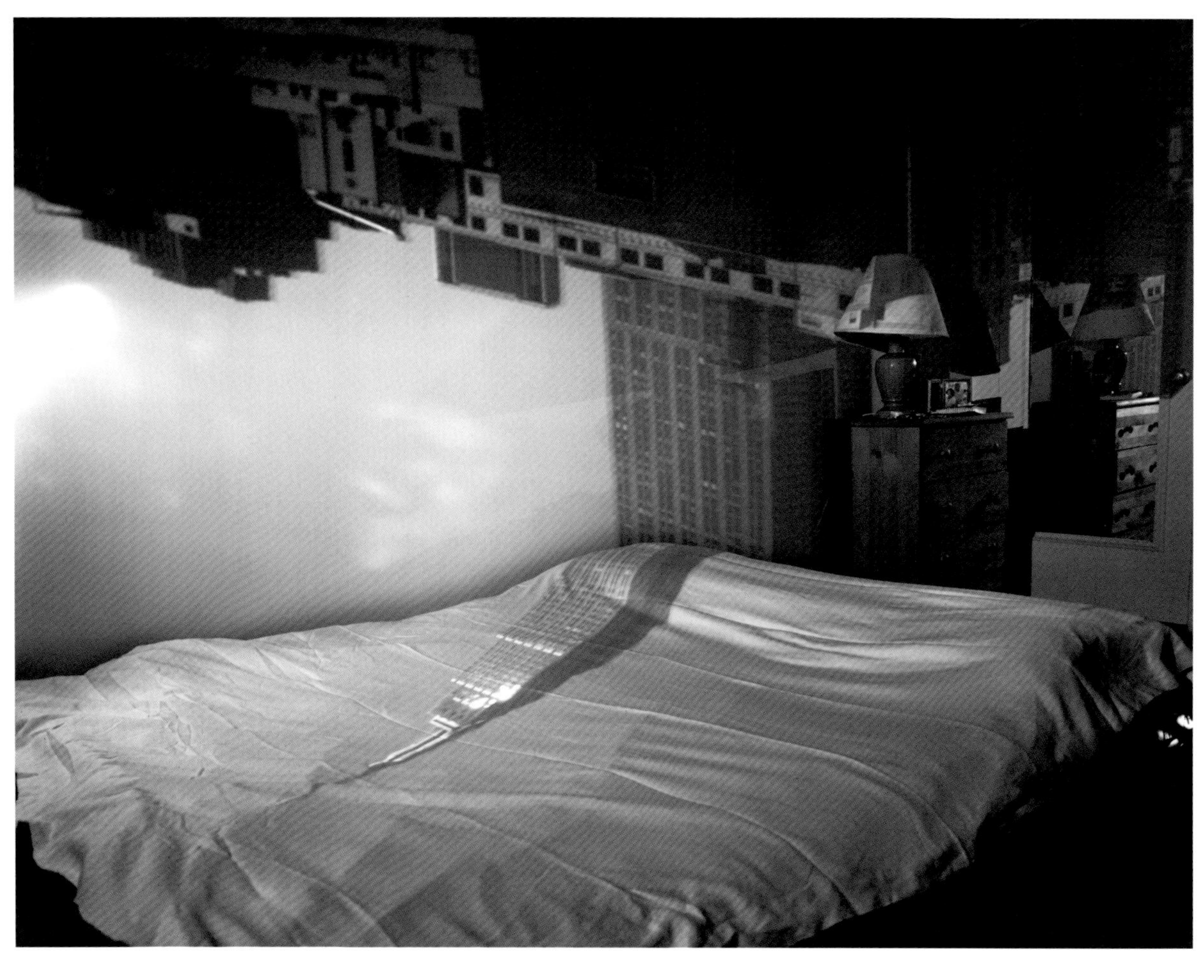

Abelardo Morell. *Camera Obscura Image of the Empire State Building in Bedroom*. 1994

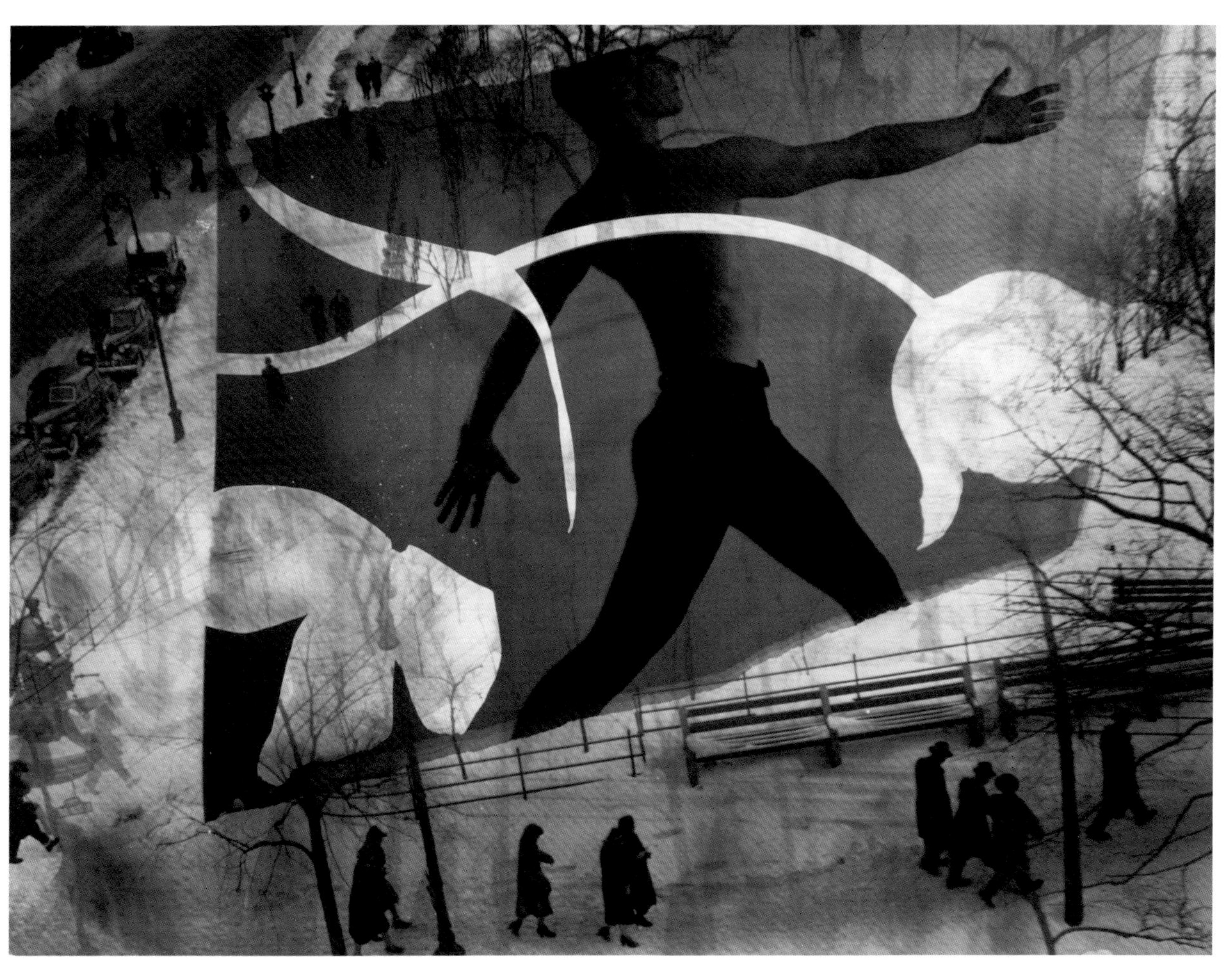

Barbara Morgan. *Spring on Madison Square*. 1938

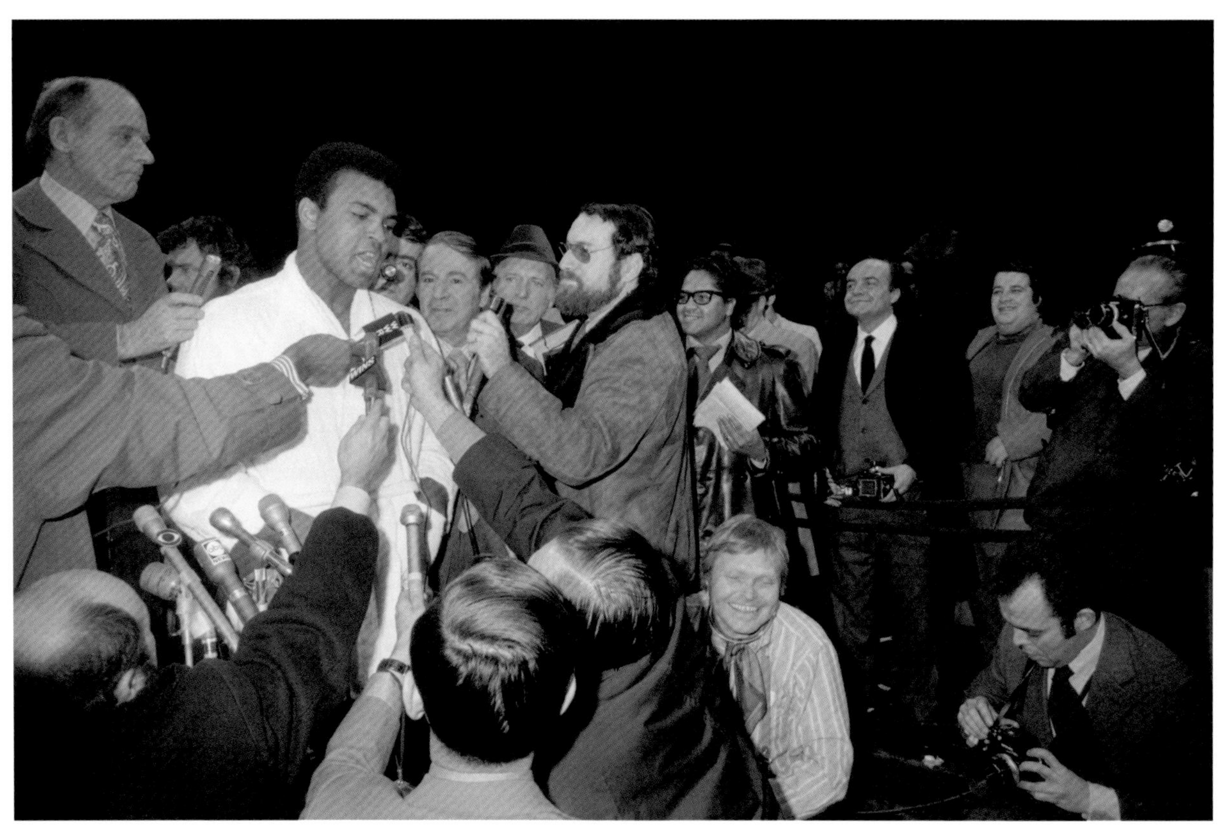

Garry Winogrand. *Muhammad Ali – Oscar Bonavena Press Conference, New York*. 1970

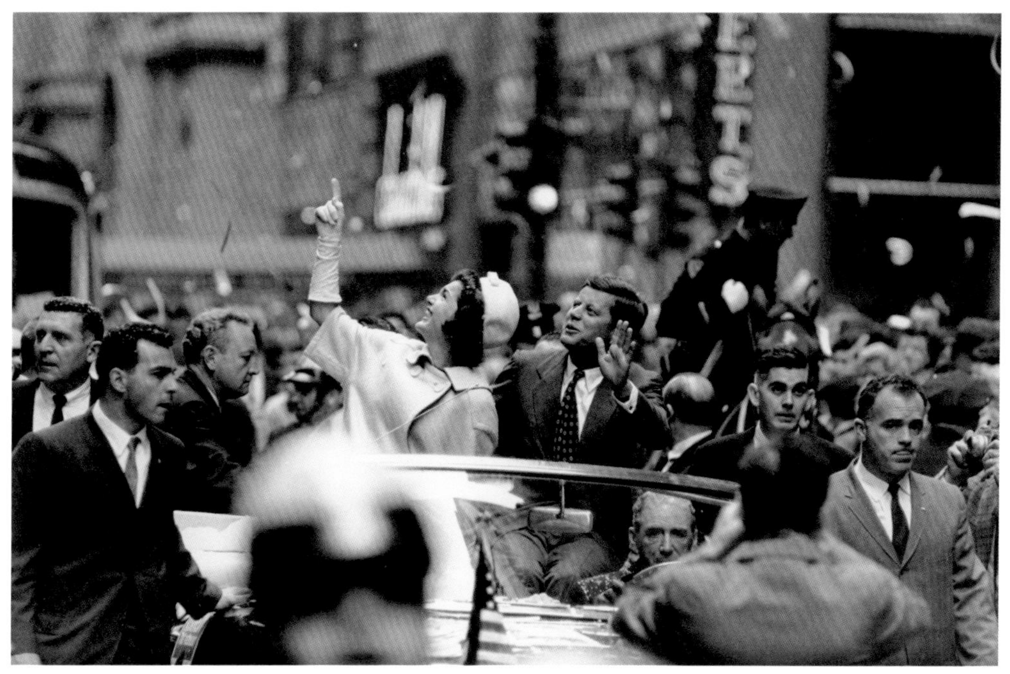

George Zimbel. *Jacqueline and John Kennedy, New York City*. 1960

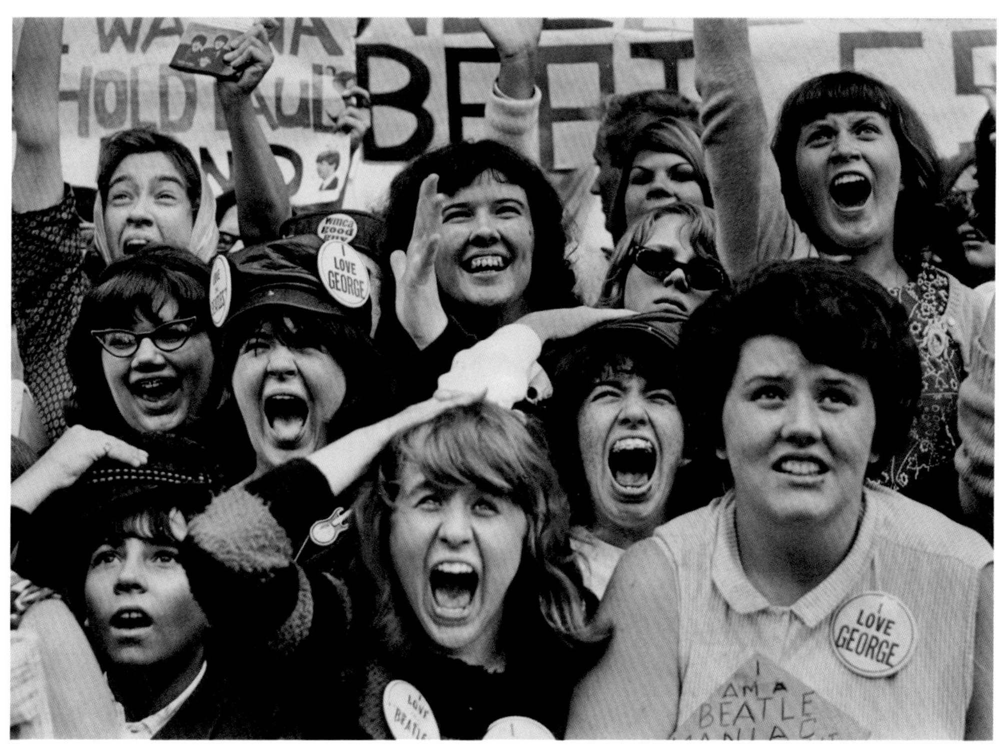

Carl T. Gosset, Jr. *Beatlemaniacs on the Loose*. August 28, 1964

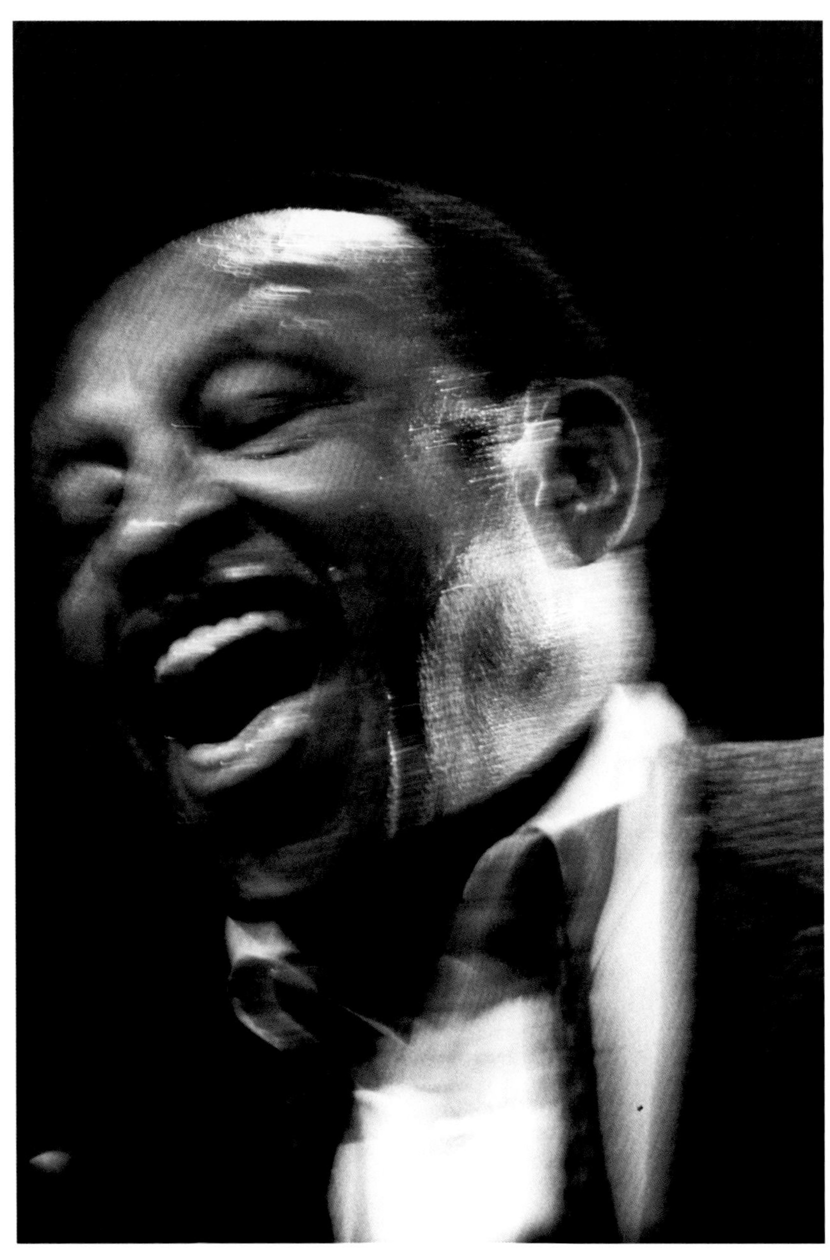

Anthony Barboza. *Lionel Hampton, Village Gate*. 1987

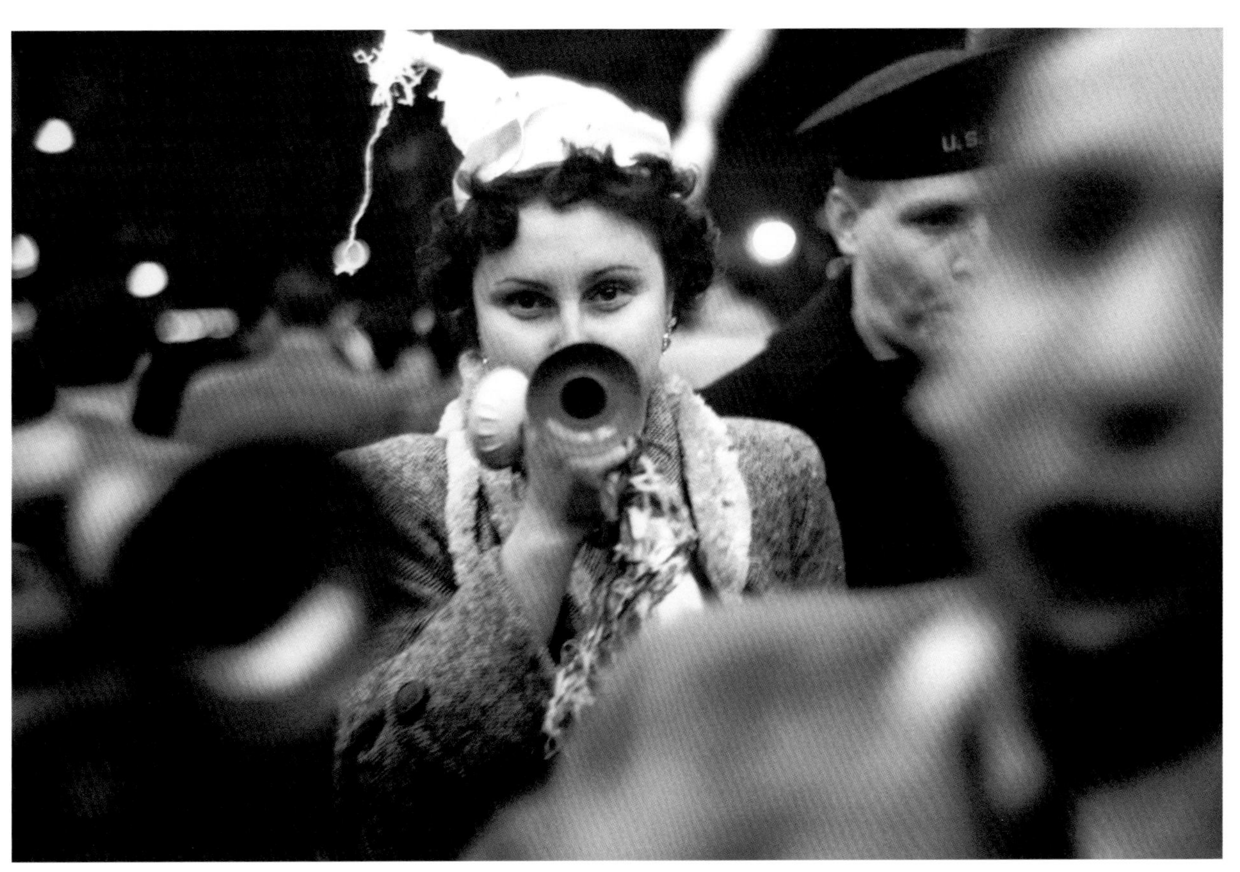

Dan Weiner. *New Year's Eve, Times Square*. 1951

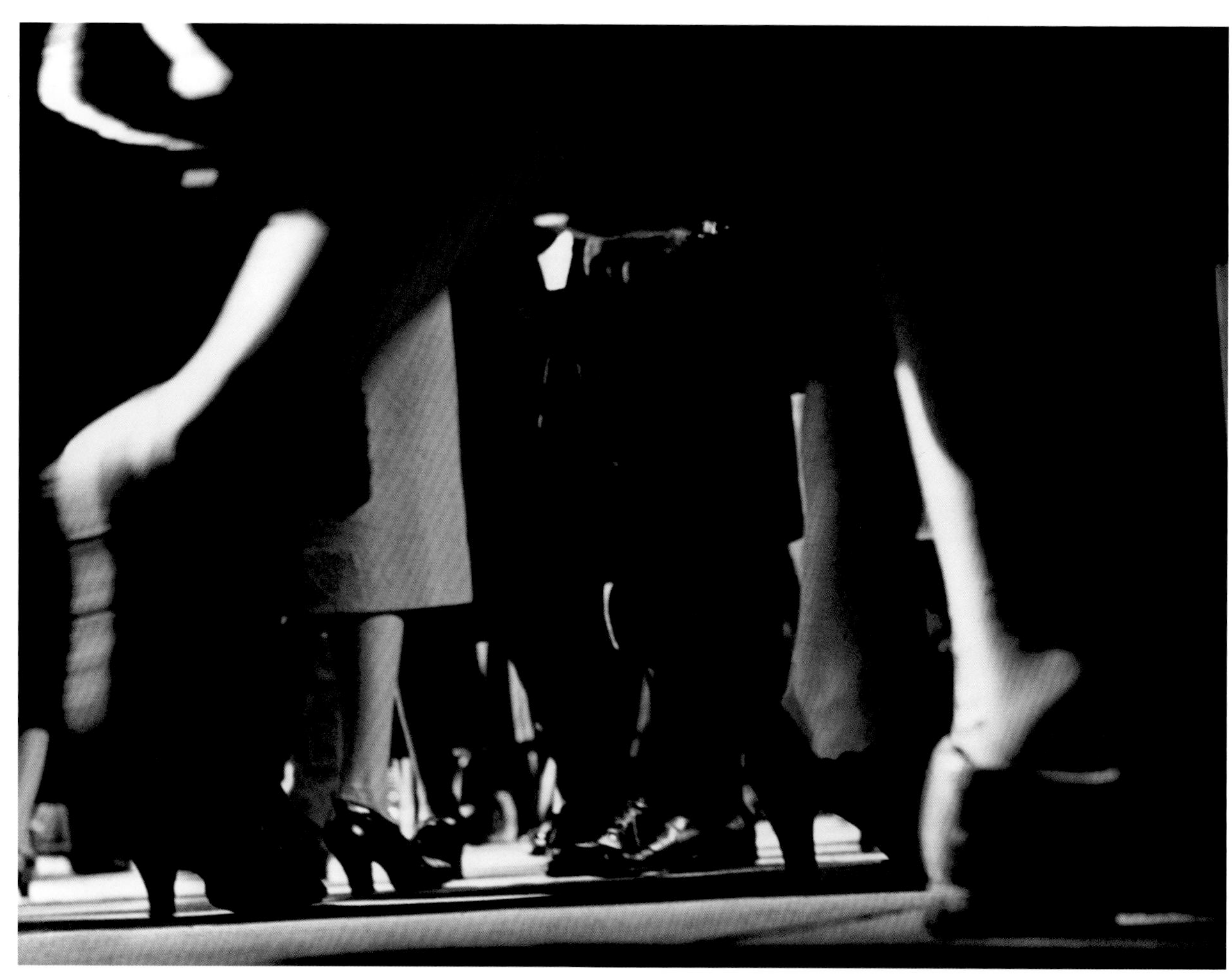

Lisette Model. *Times Square*. 1940

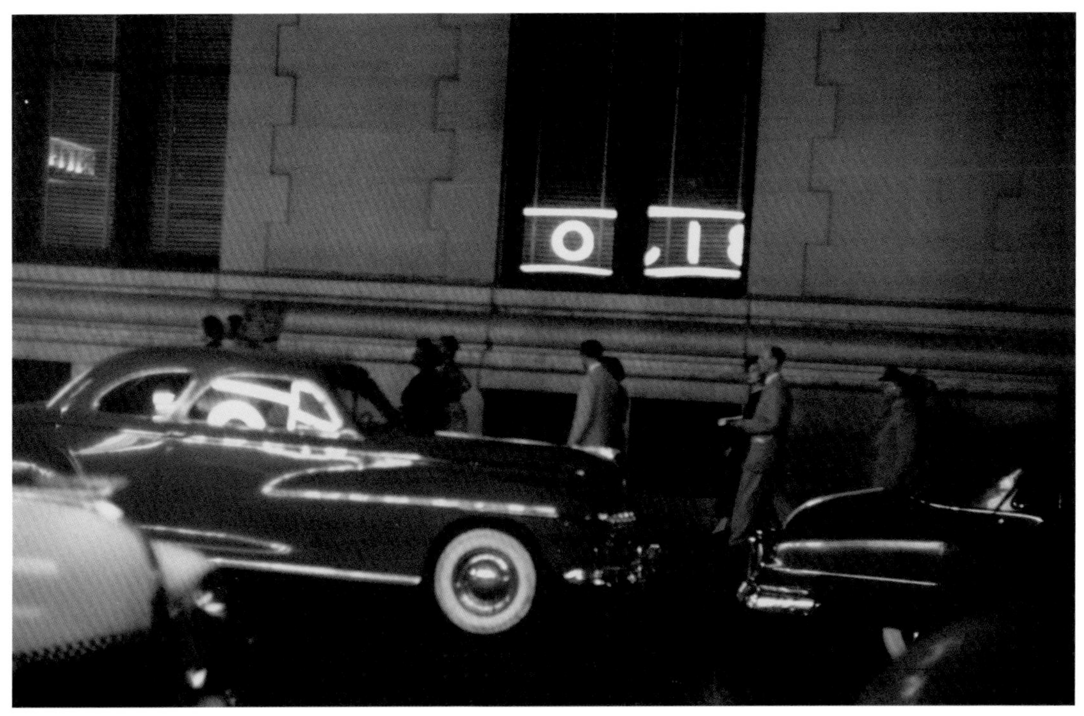

Louis Faurer. *New York*. 1950

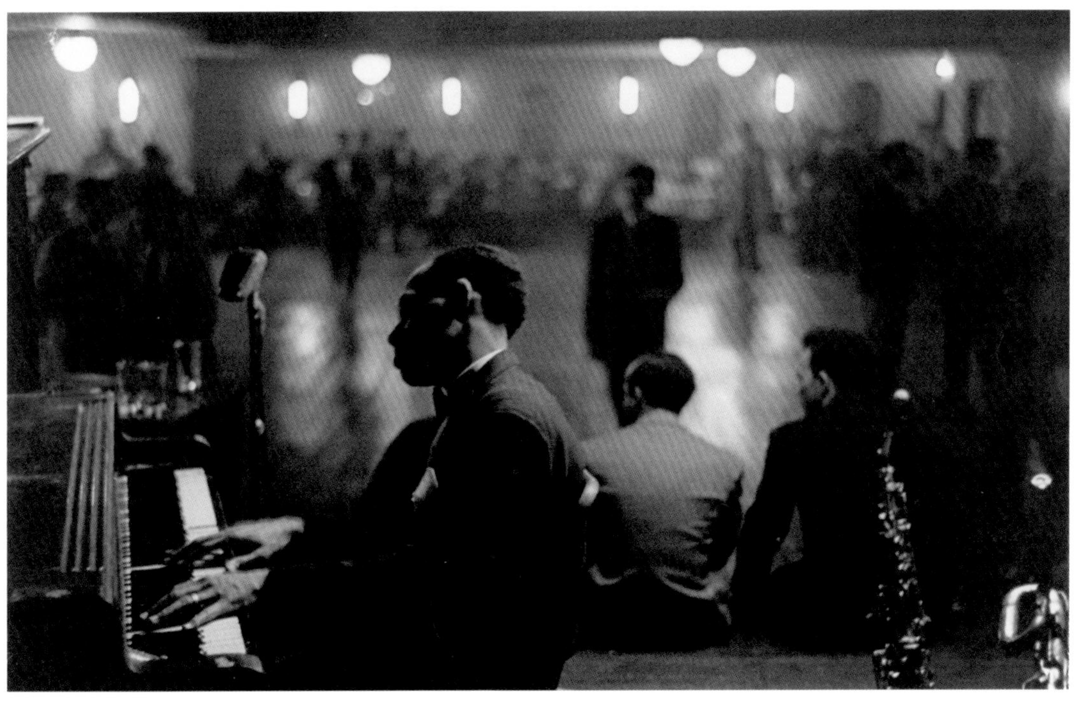

Ed Feingersh. *Dance Hall, New York*. c. 1953

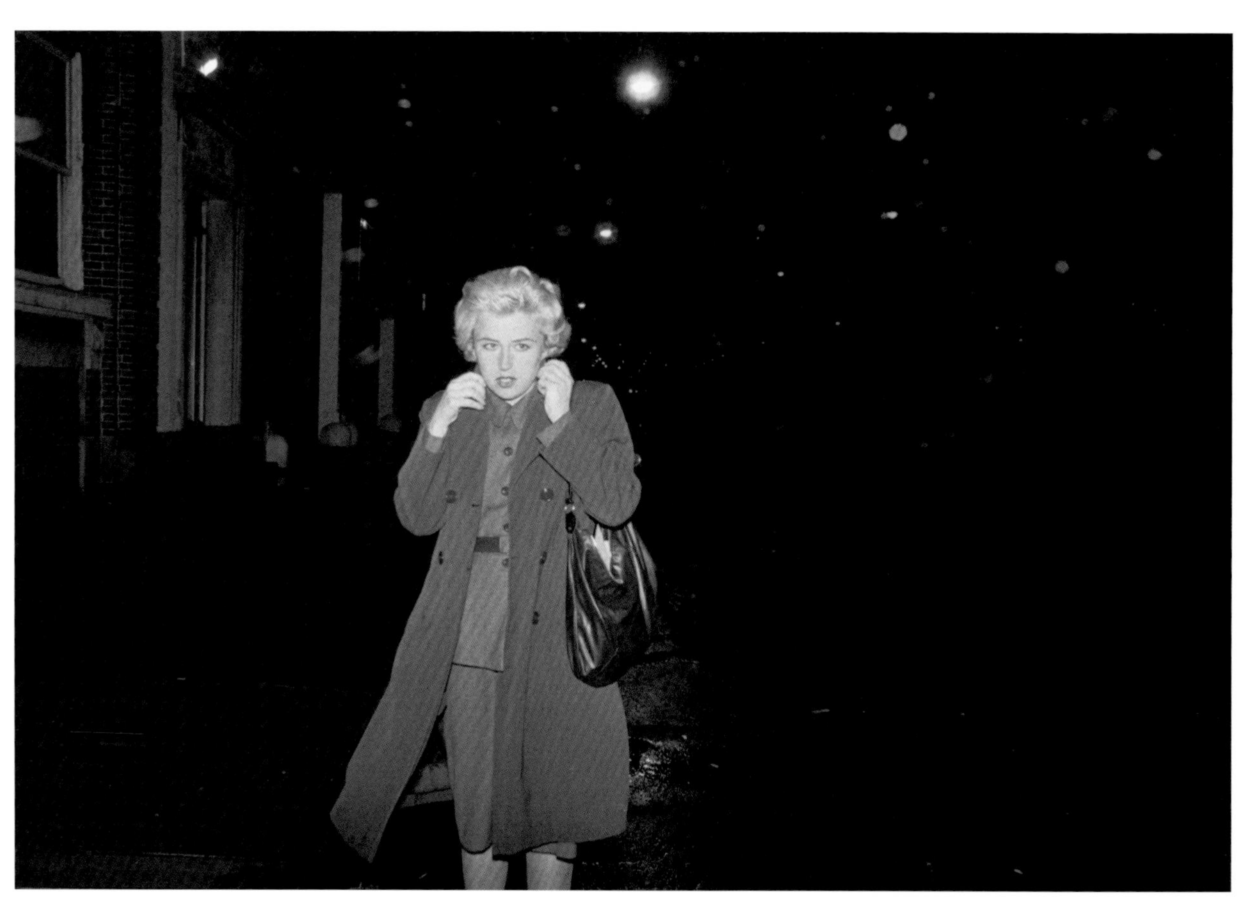

Cindy Sherman. *Untitled Film Still #54*. 1980

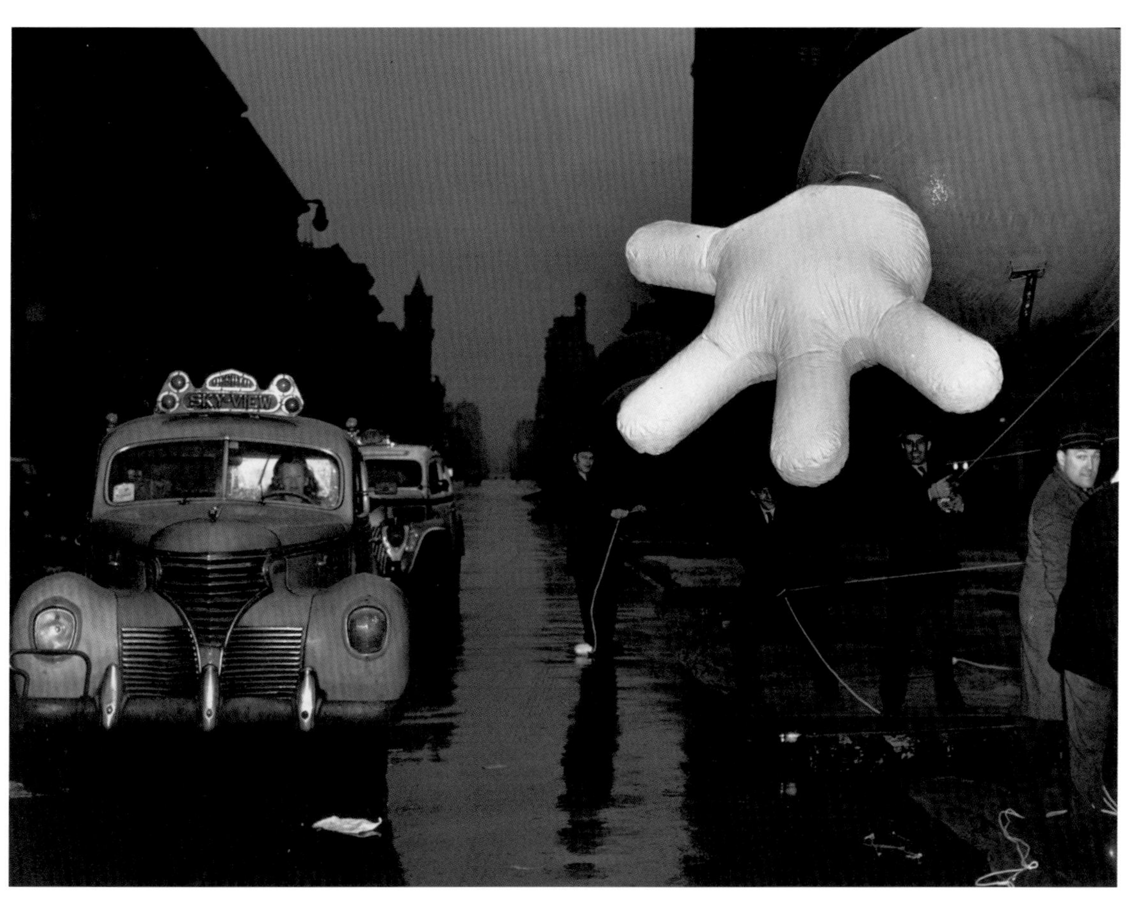

Weegee. *Macy's Thanksgiving Day Parade*. c. 1942

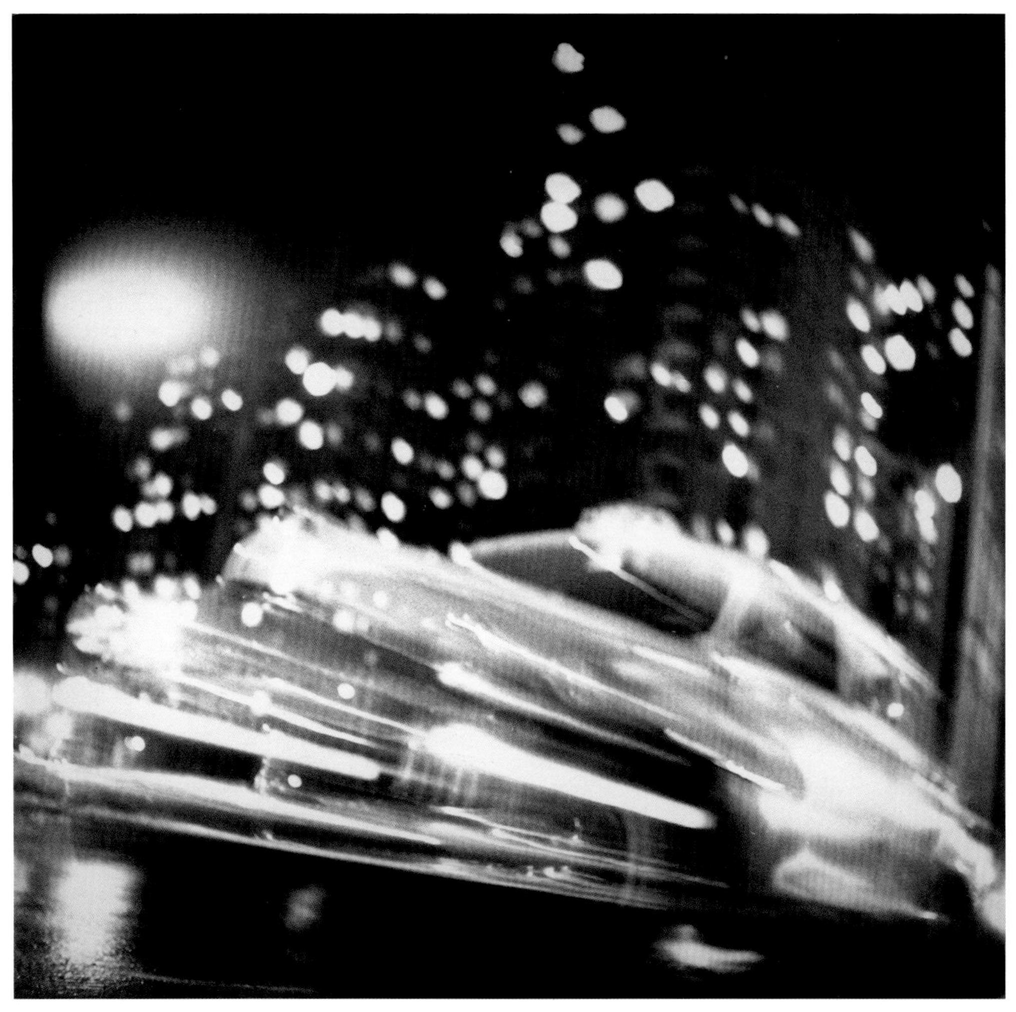

Ted Croner. *Taxi—New York—Night*. 1947–48

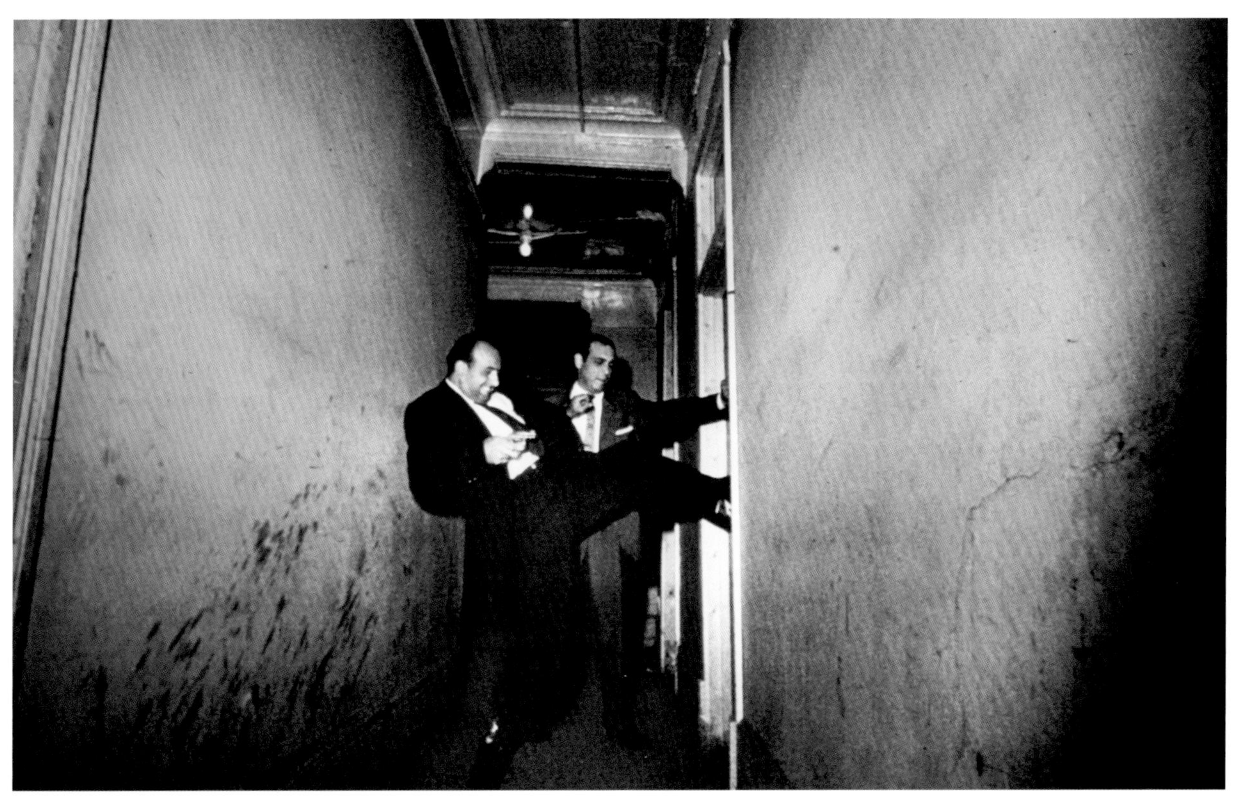

Gordon Parks. From the photostory "The Atmosphere of Crime," *Life* magazine. September 9, 1957

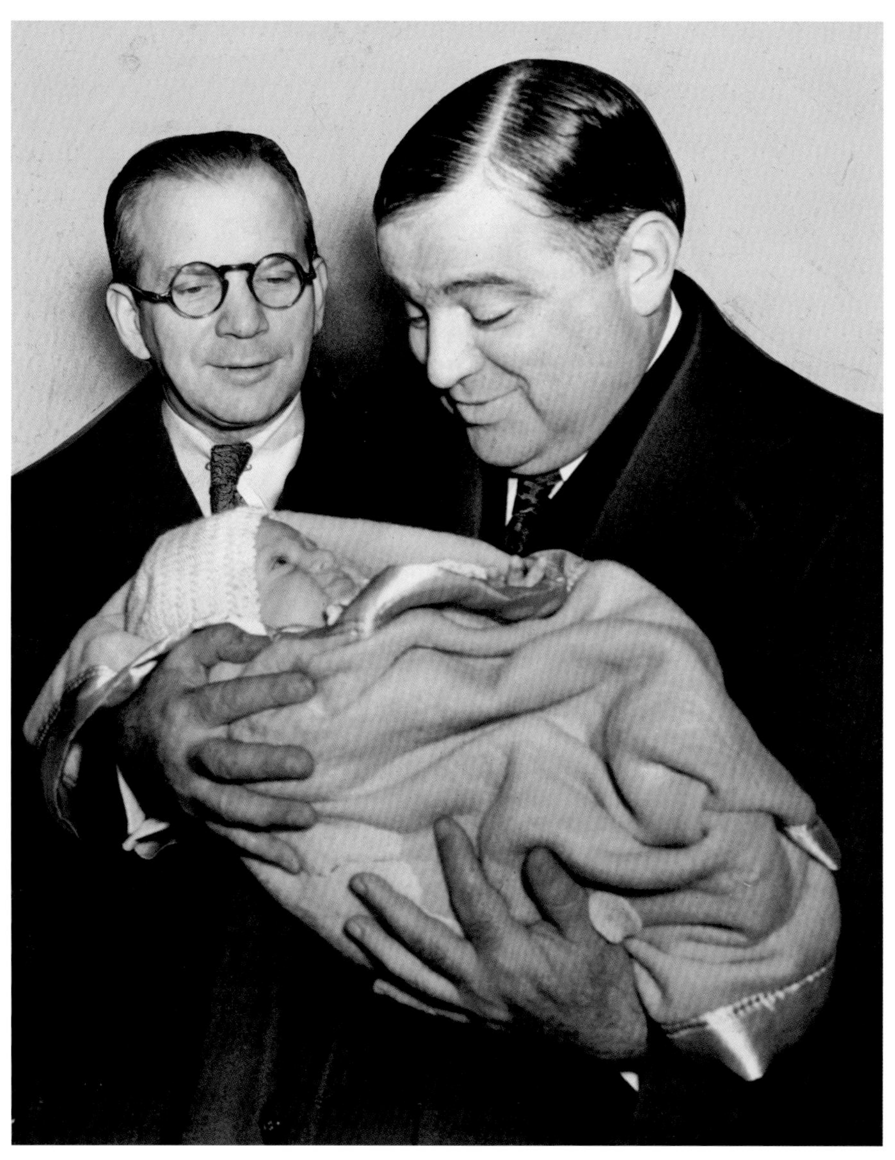

Times Wide World Photos. *The Mayor and a Baby Exchange Smiles*. December 8, 1938

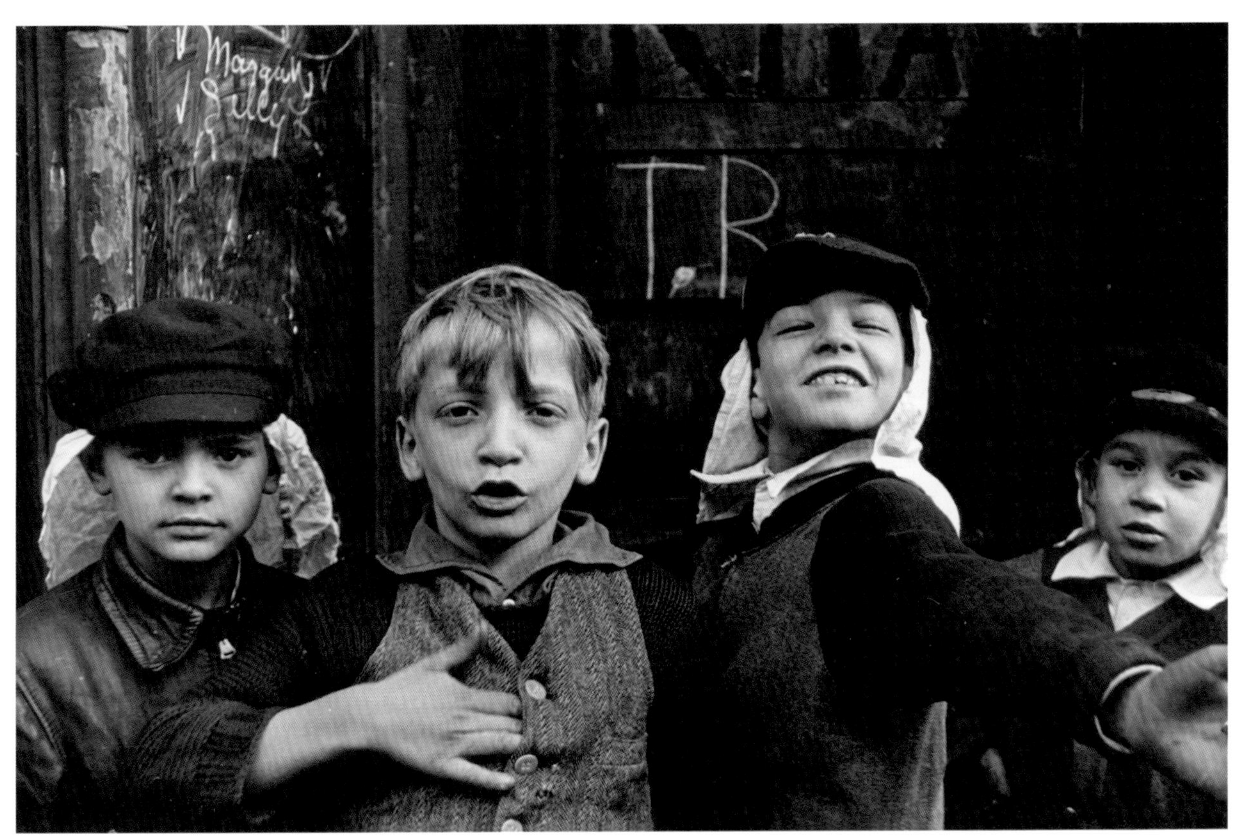

Helen Levitt. *New York*. c. 1940

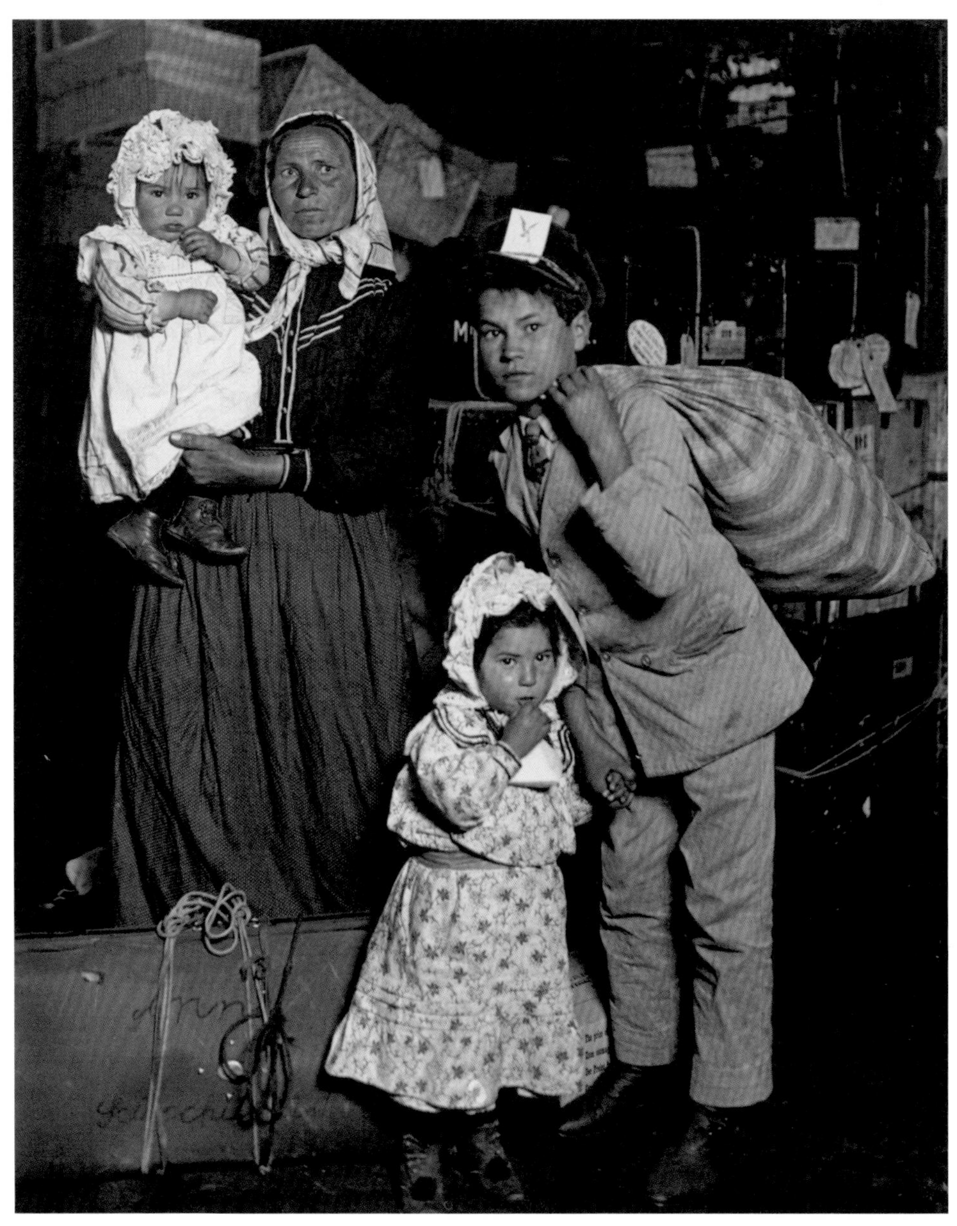

Lewis W. Hine. *Italian Family Looking for Lost Baggage, Ellis Island, New York*. 1905

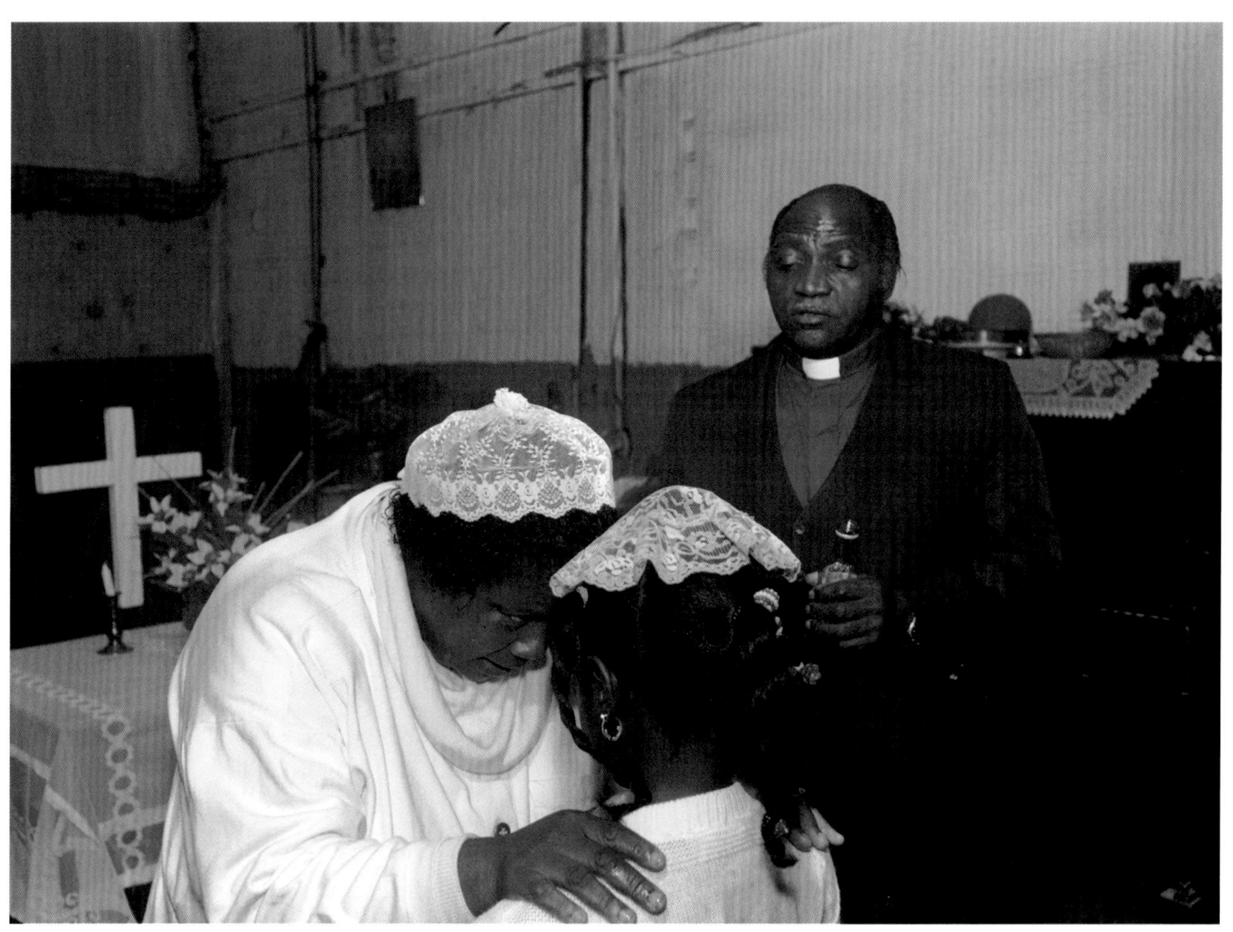

Thomas Roma. *Untitled* from the series *Come Sunday*. 1991–94

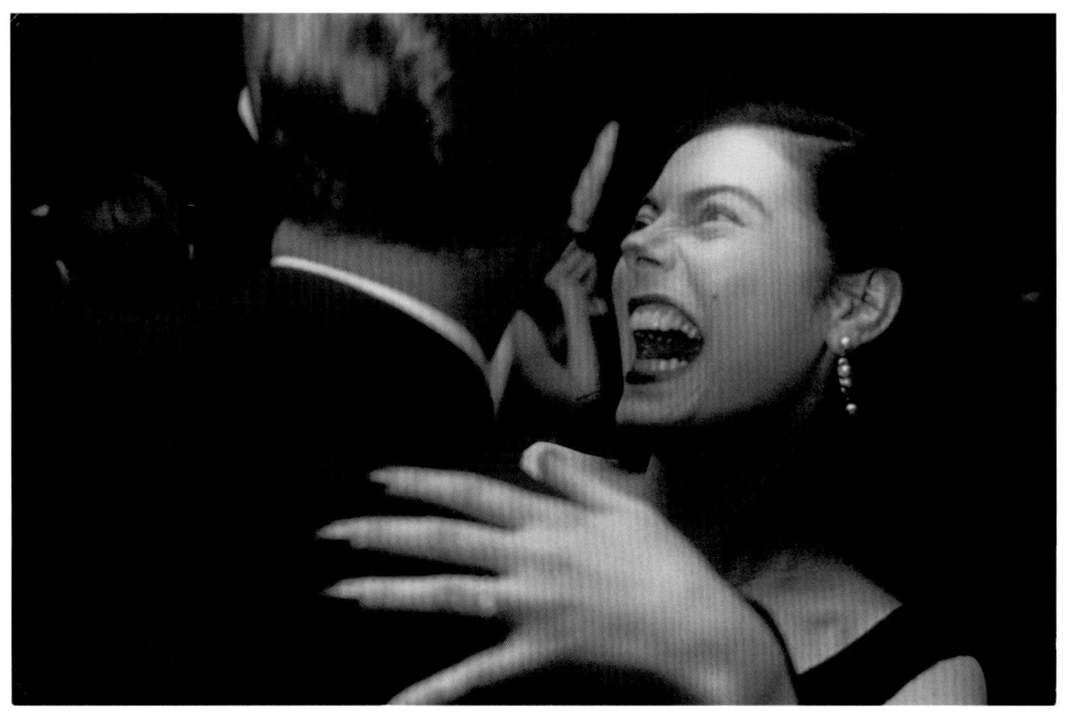

Garry Winogrand. *El Morocco*. 1955

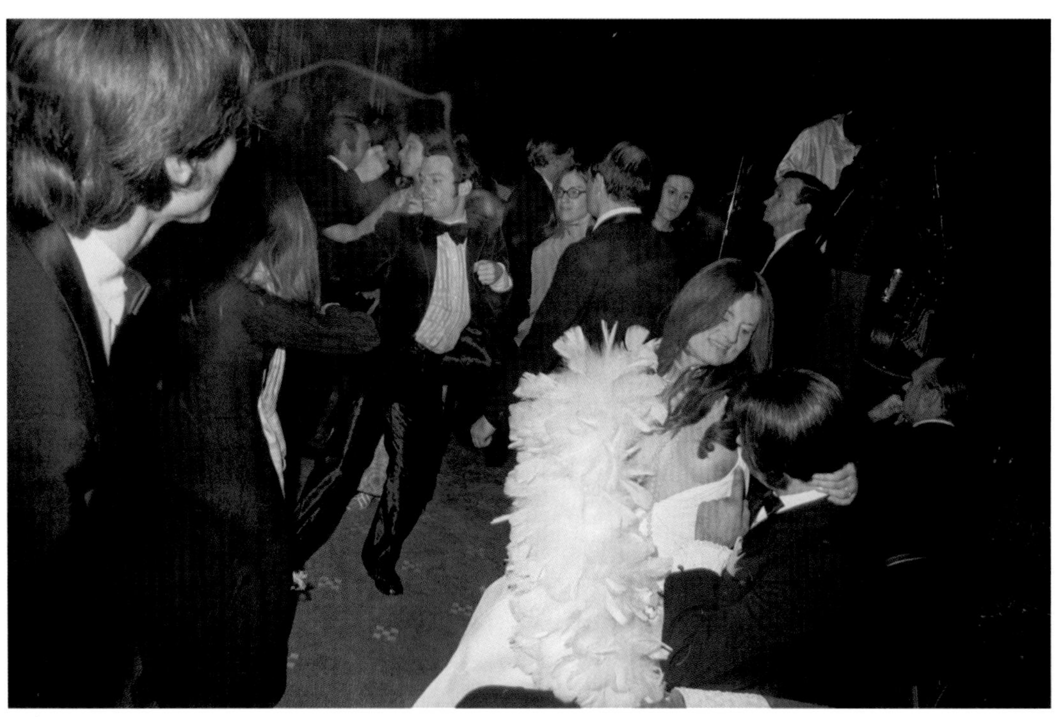

Garry Winogrand. *Metropolitan Museum of Art Centennial Ball, New York*. 1969

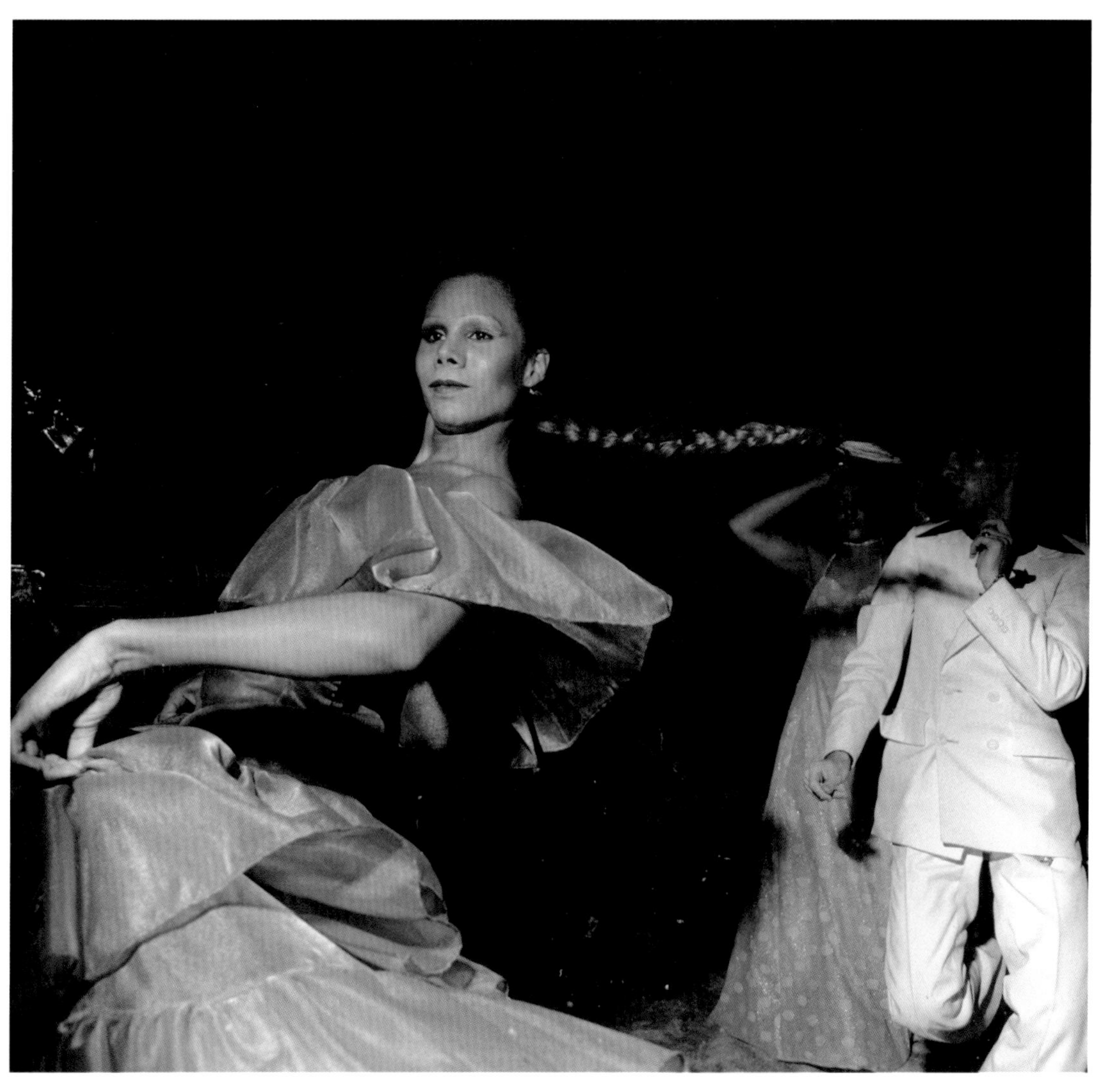

Larry Fink. *Studio 54, New York City*. May 1977

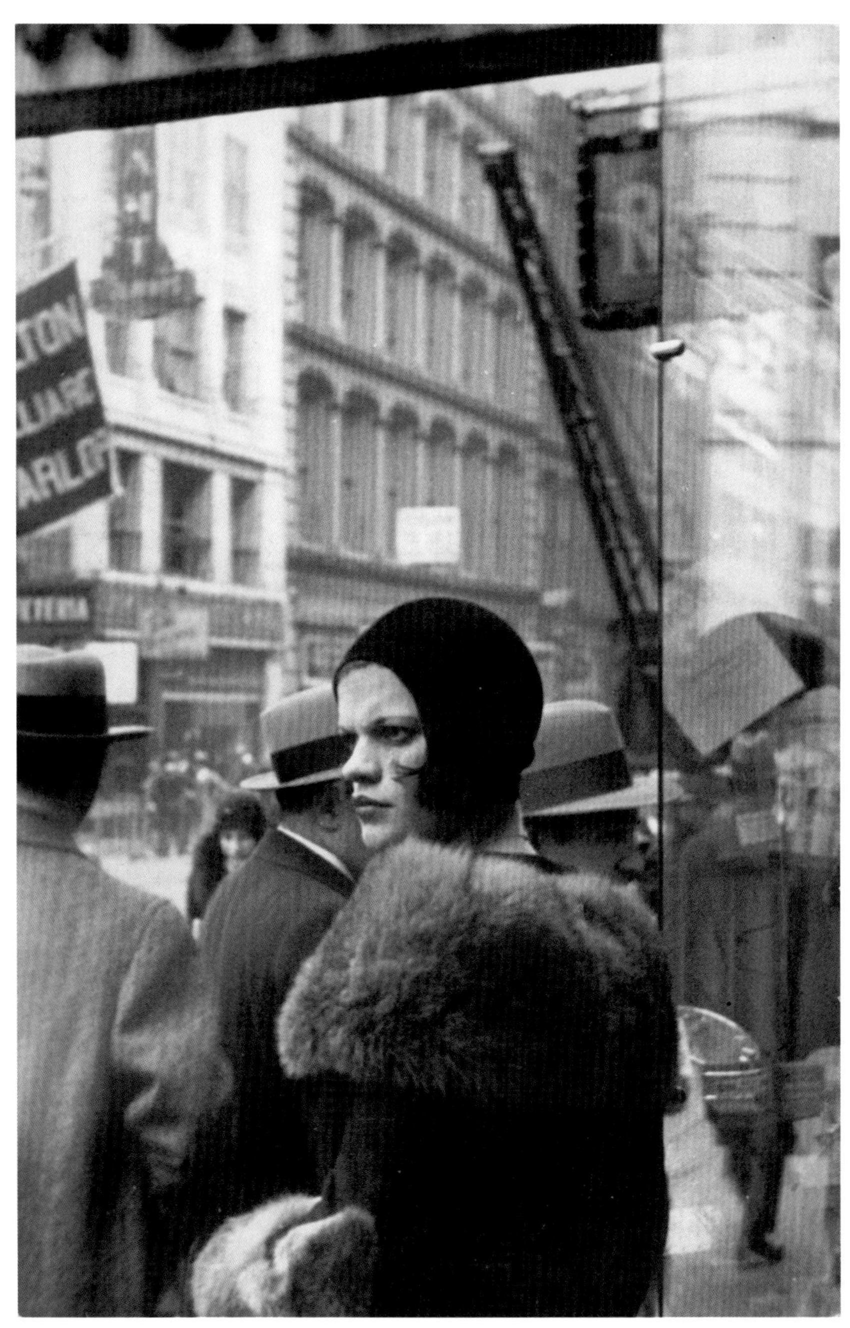

Walker Evans. *Girl in Fulton Street, New York*. 1929

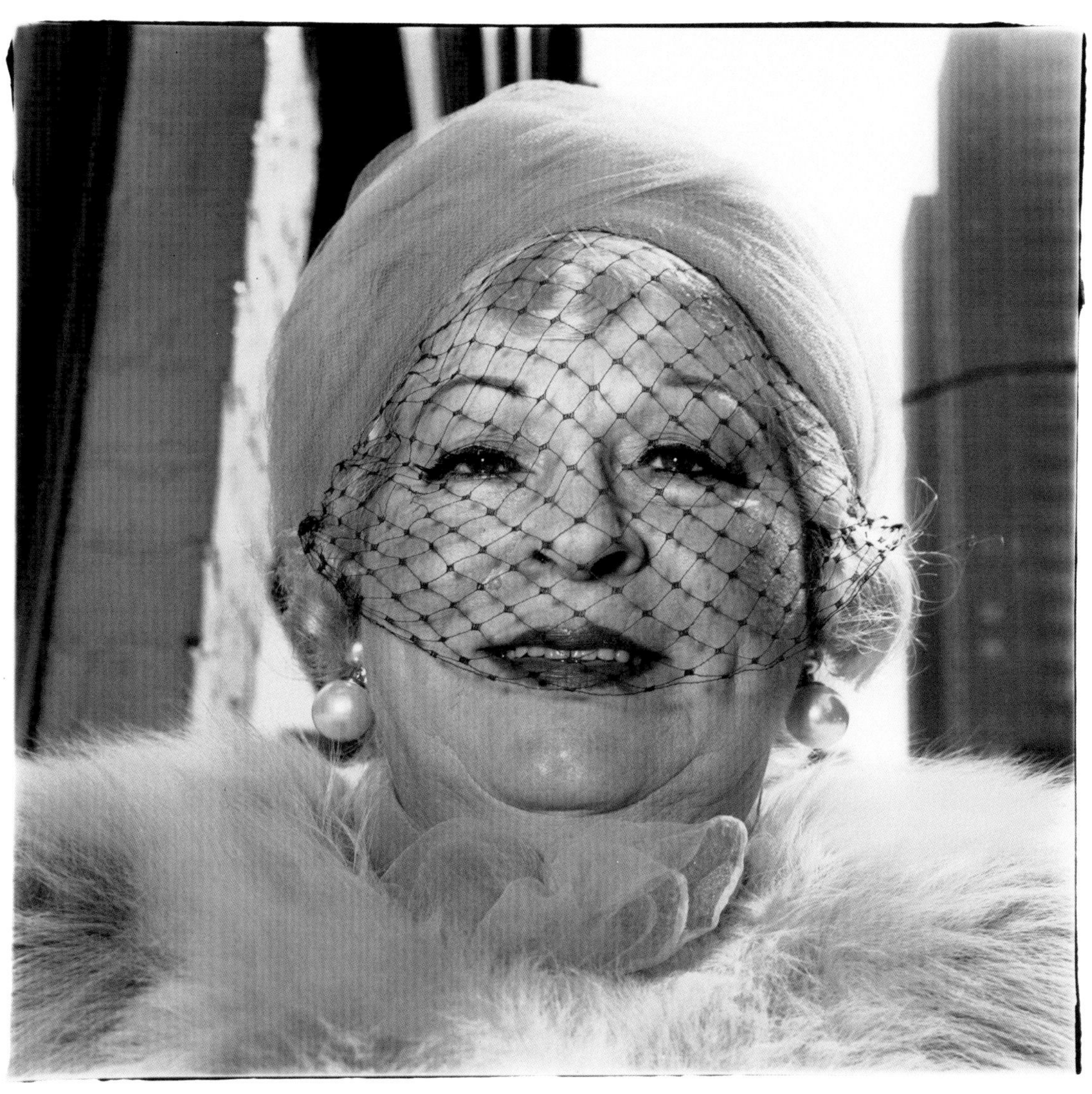

Diane Arbus. *Woman with a Veil on Fifth Avenue, New York City*. 1968

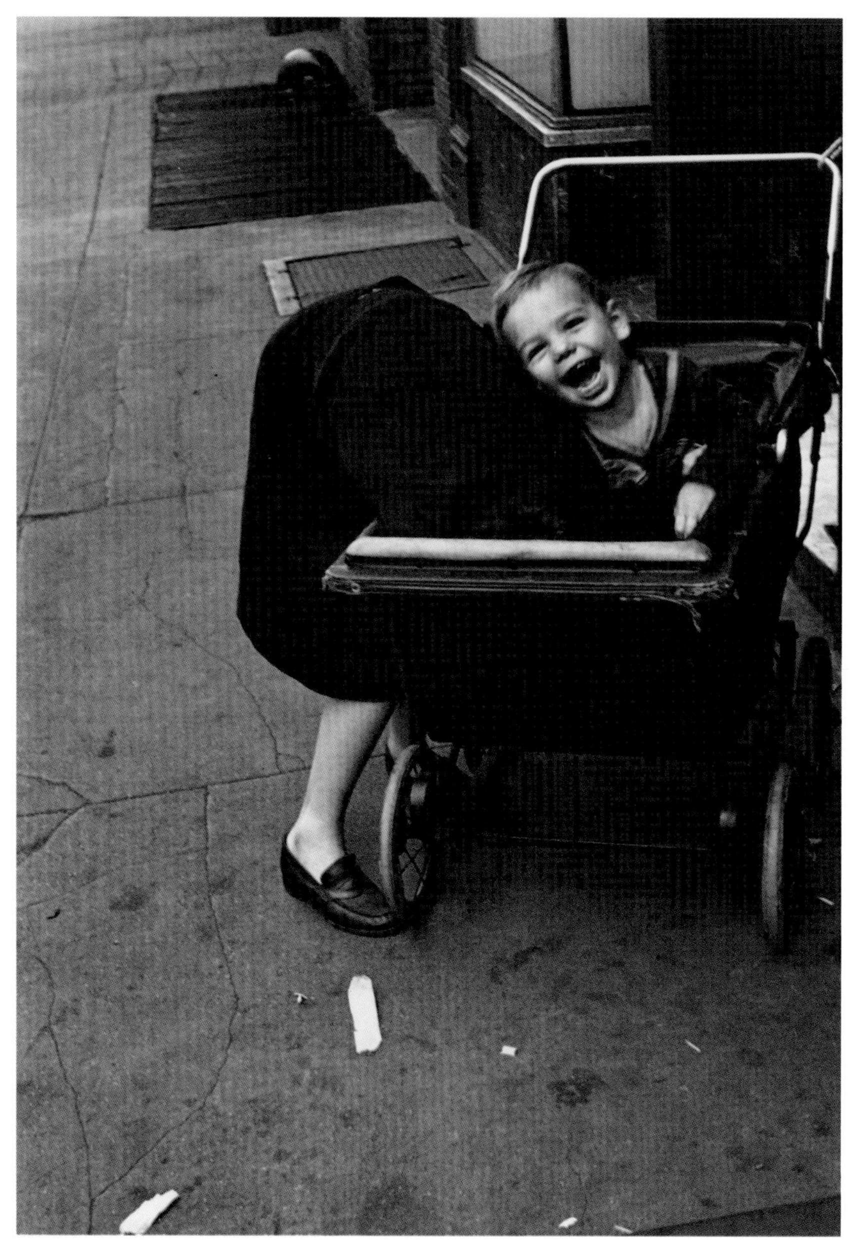

Helen Levitt. *New York*. c. 1945

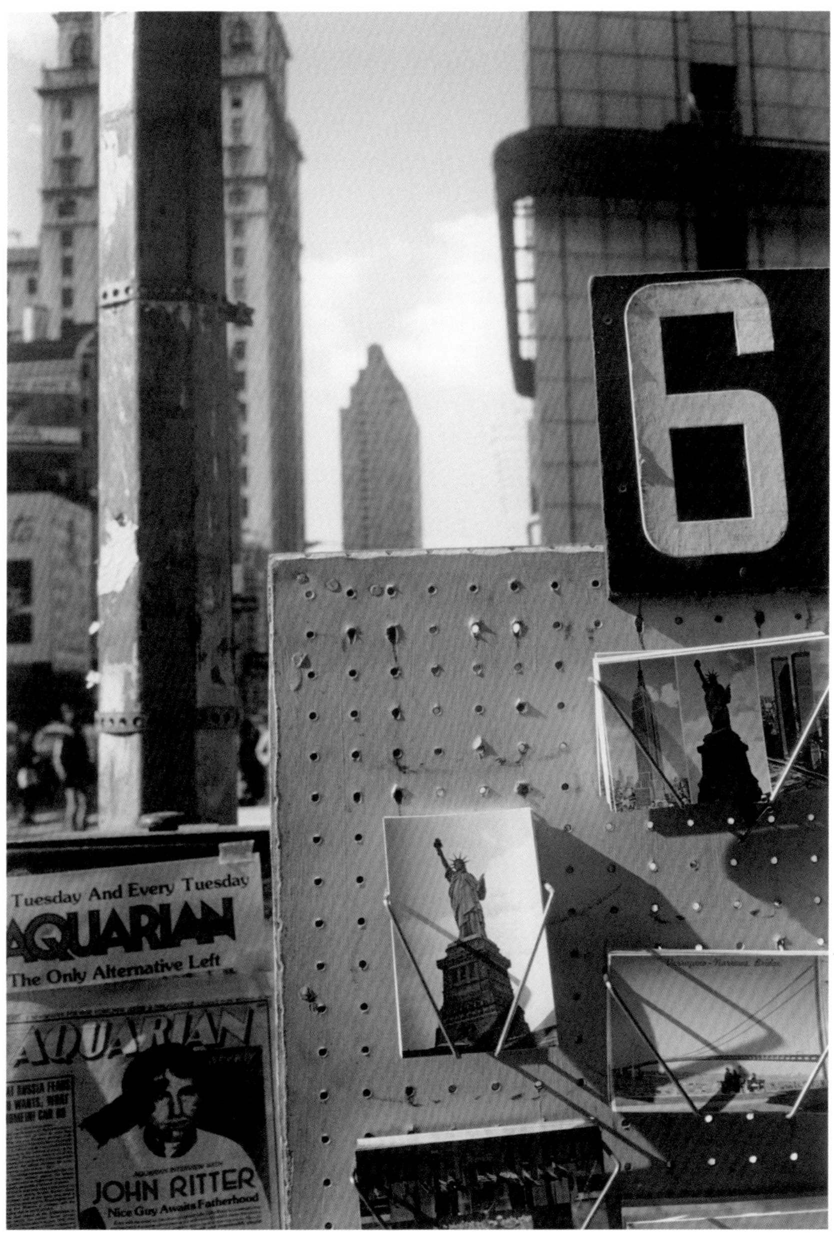

Lee Friedlander. *New York City*. 1980

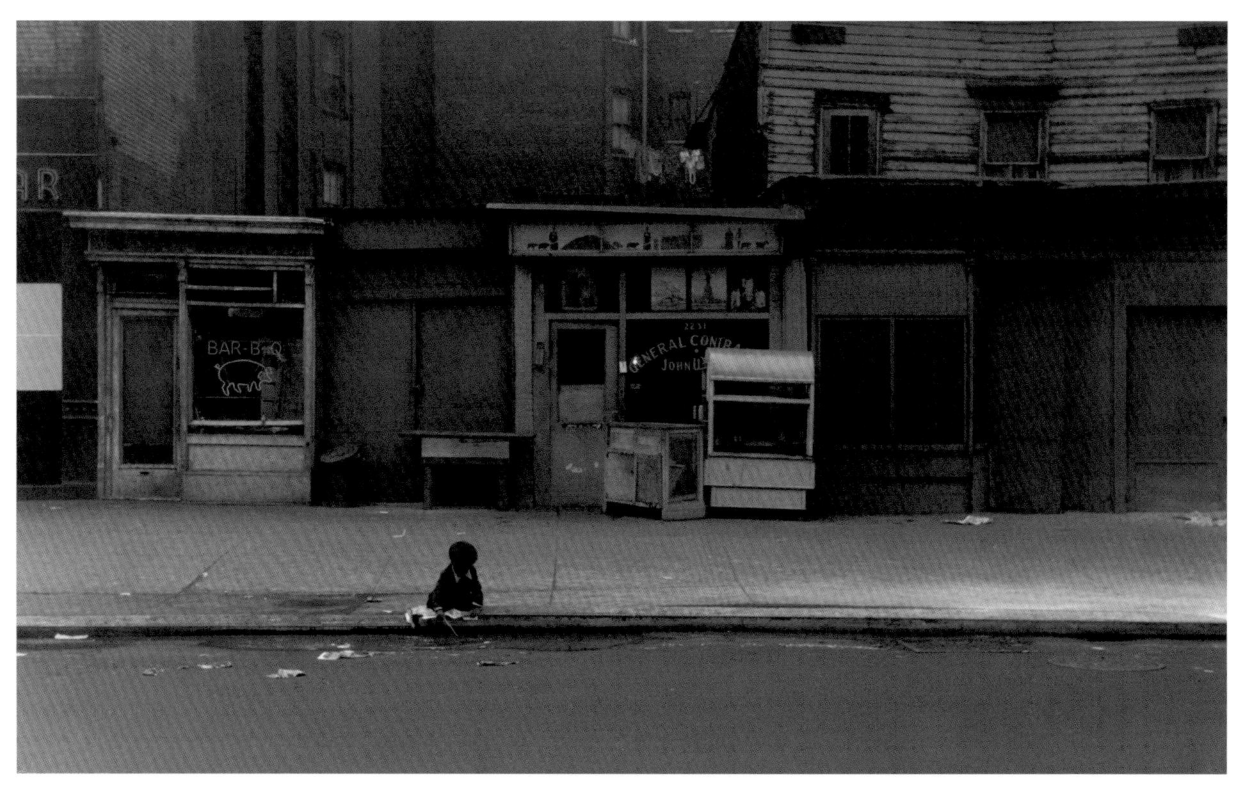

Roy DeCarava. *Child Playing at Curb, Eighth Avenue*. 1952

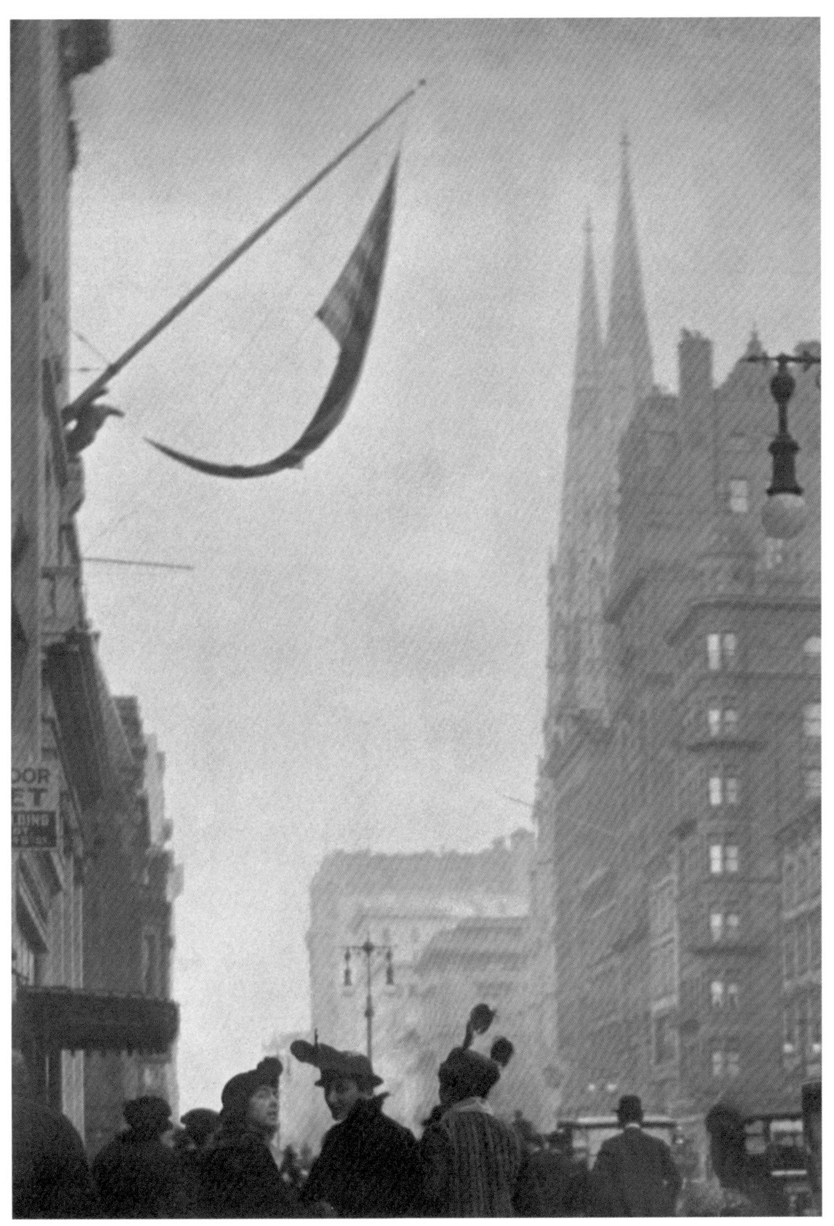

Paul Strand. *Fifth Avenue, New York*. 1915

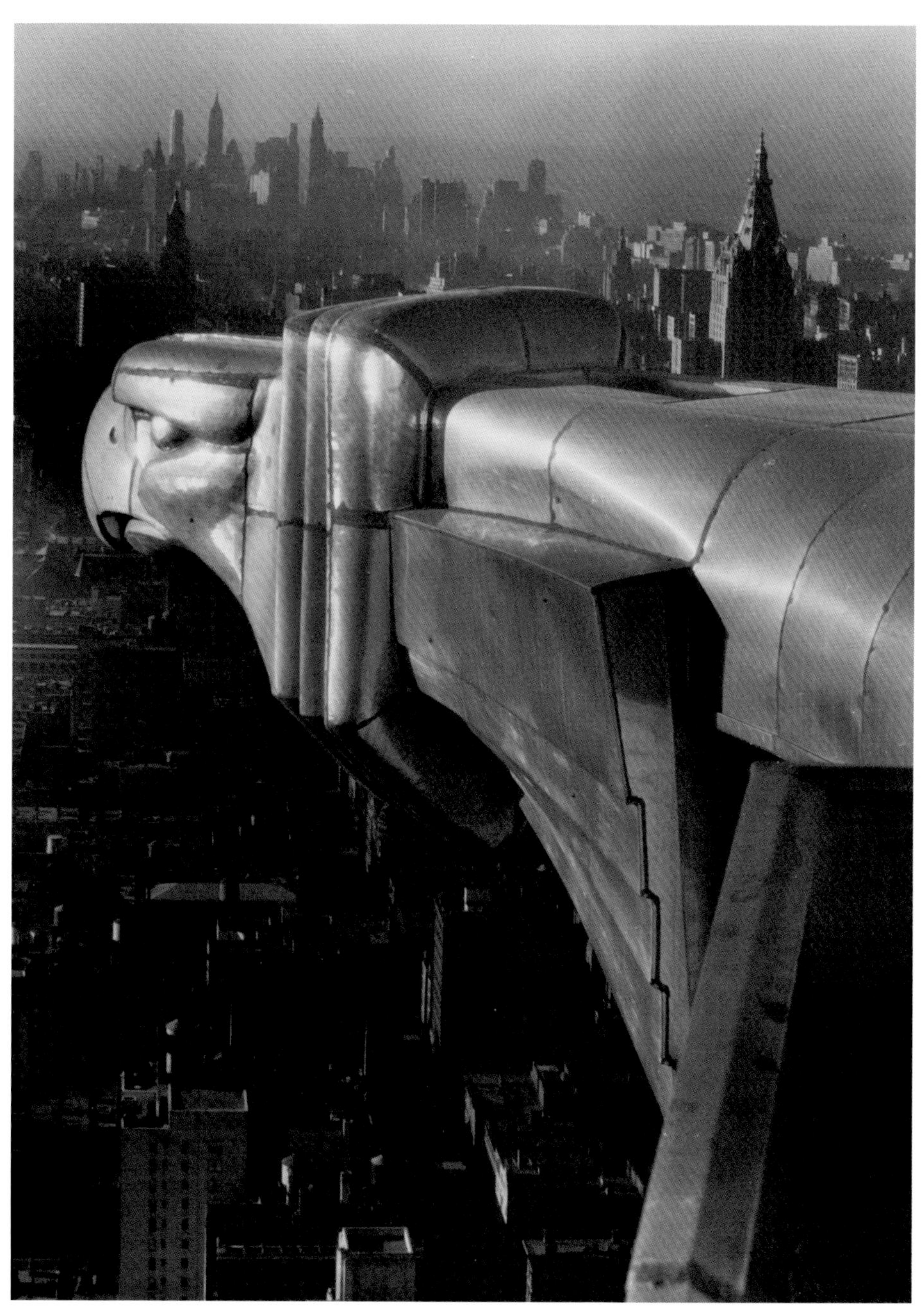

Margaret Bourke-White. *Ornamental Gargoyle, Chrysler Building*. 1934

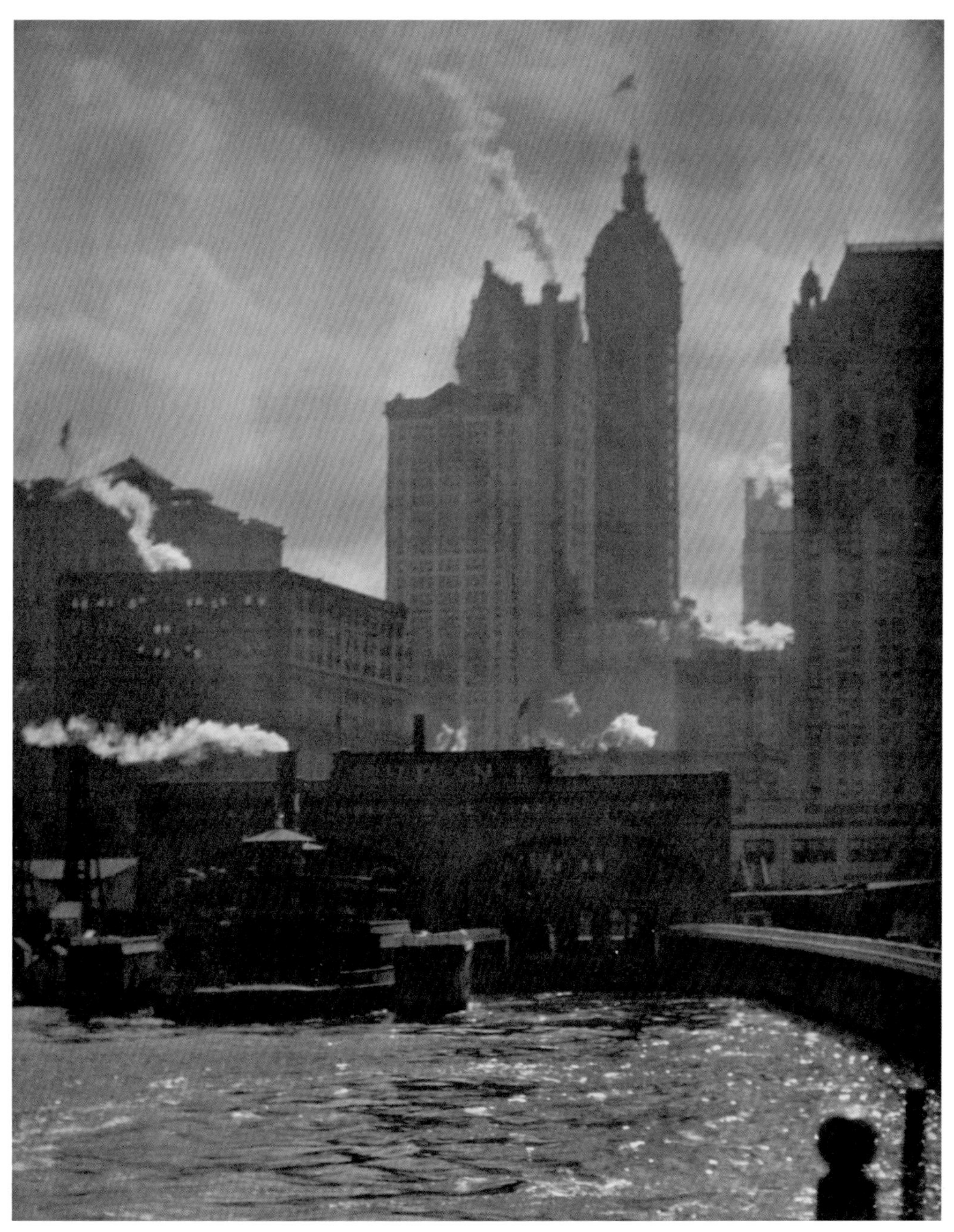

Alfred Stieglitz. *City of Ambition*. 1910

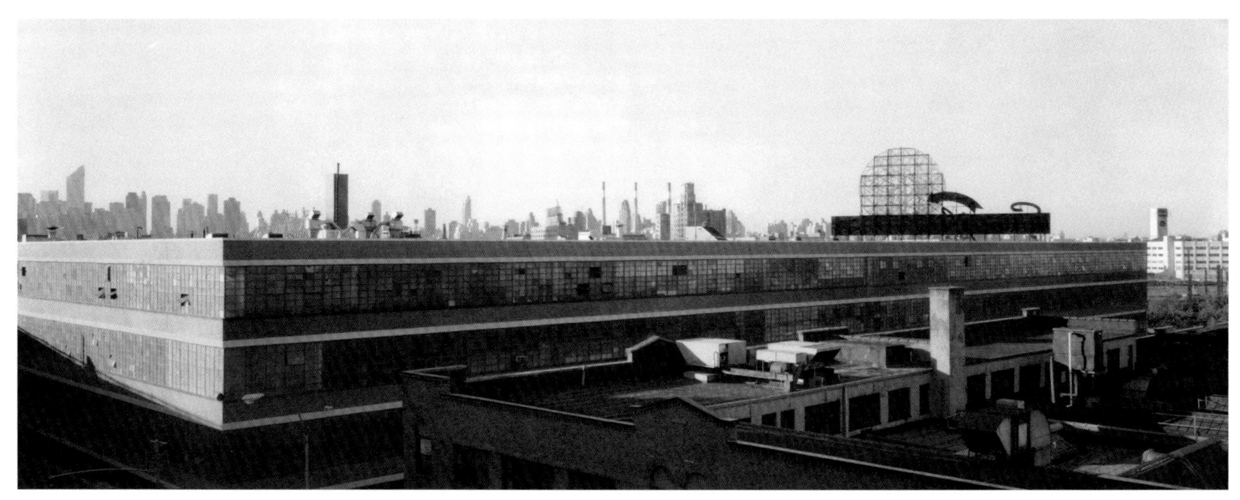

Lois Conner. *Queens, New York*. 1990

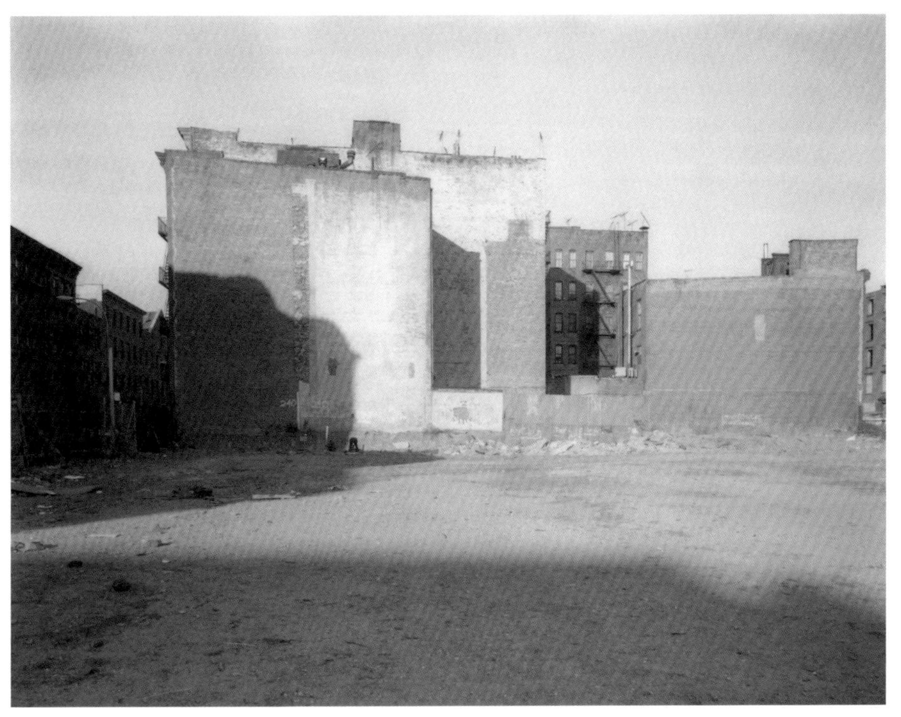

Jan Groover. *Untitled*. 1981

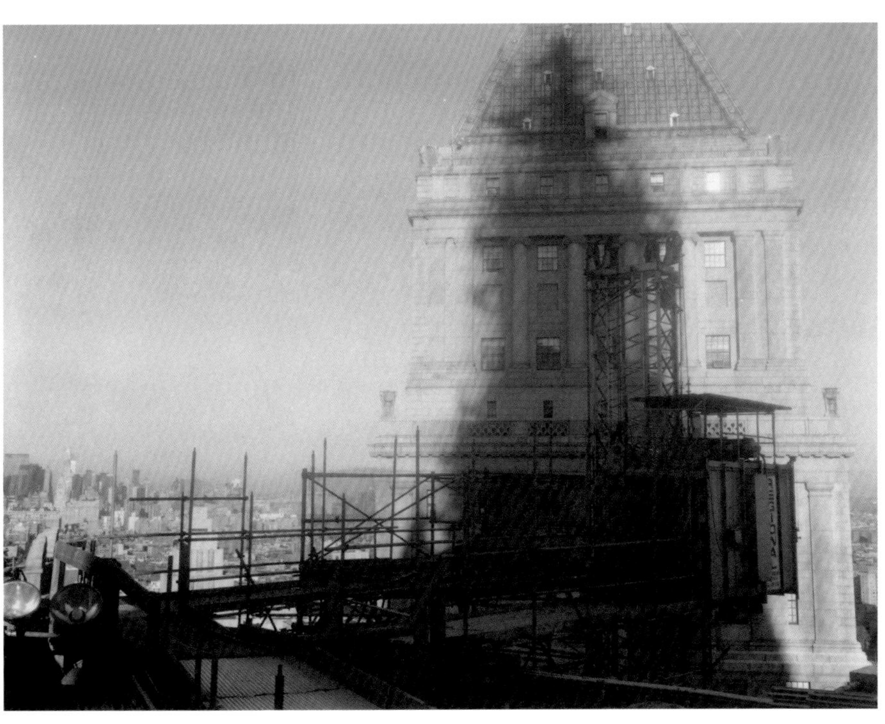

Madoka Takagi. *North View from Municipal Building*. 1991

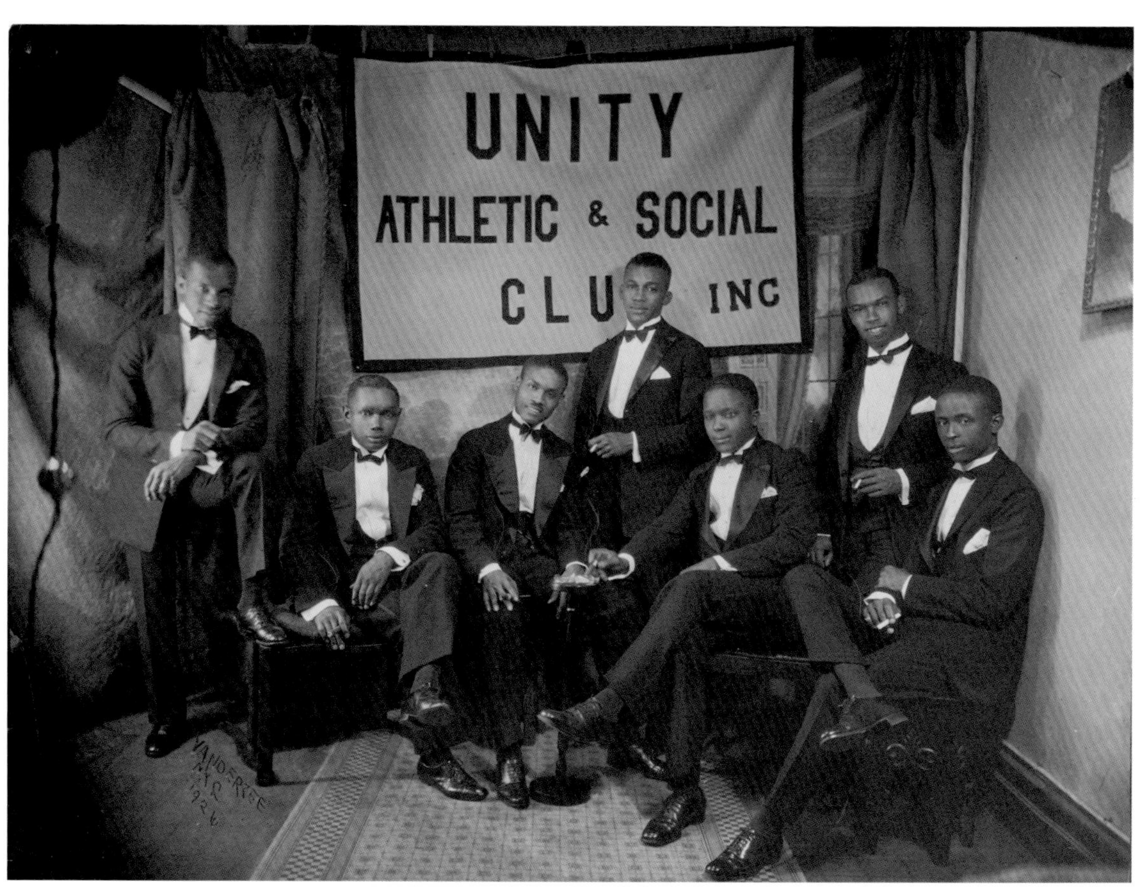

James Van Der Zee. *Unity Athletic and Social Club, Inc.* 1926

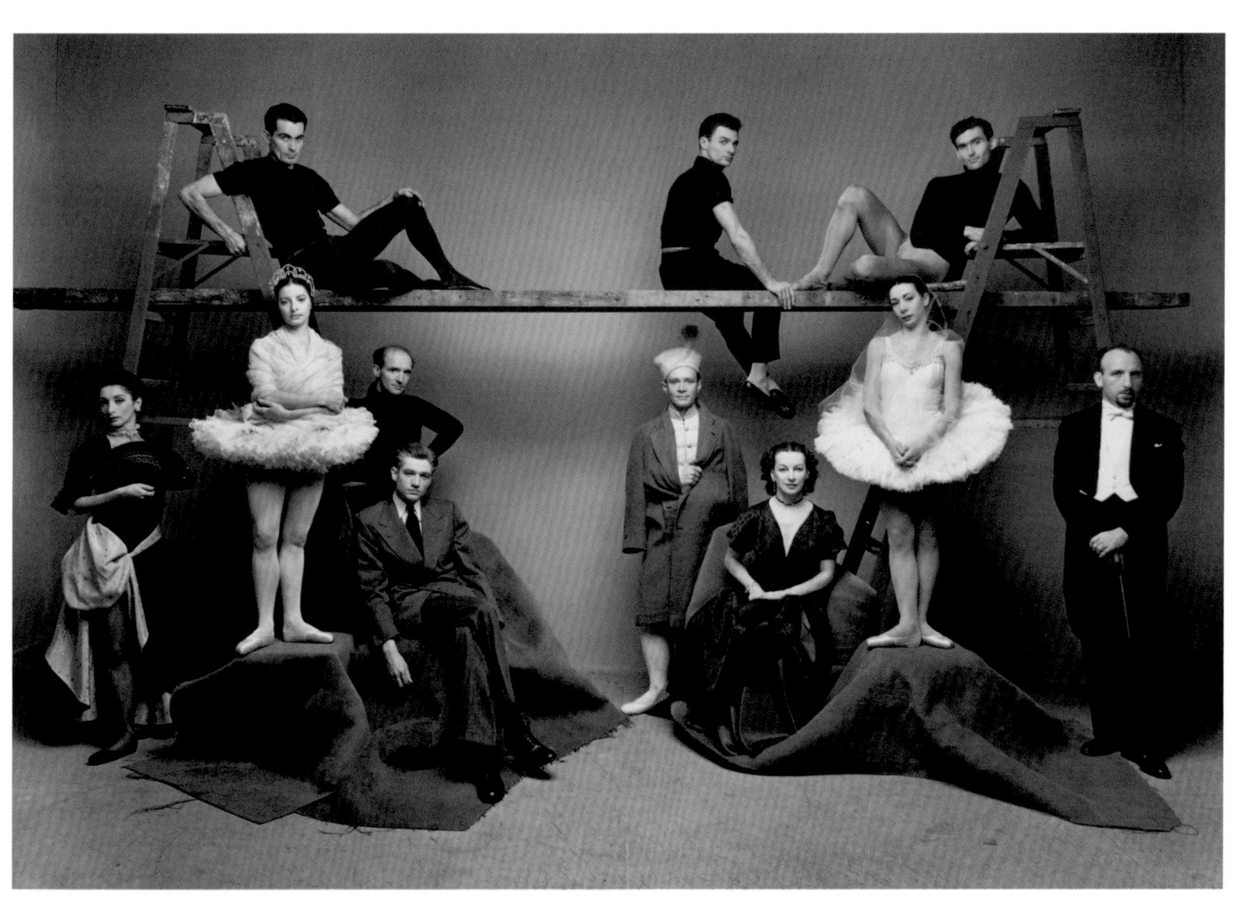

Irving Penn. *Ballet Theatre, New York*. 1947

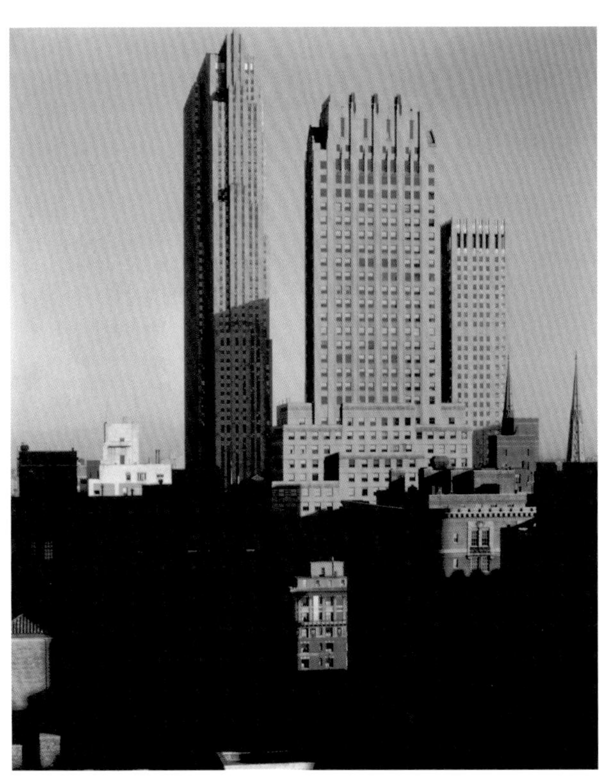

Alfred Stieglitz. *From the Shelton, West*. 1935

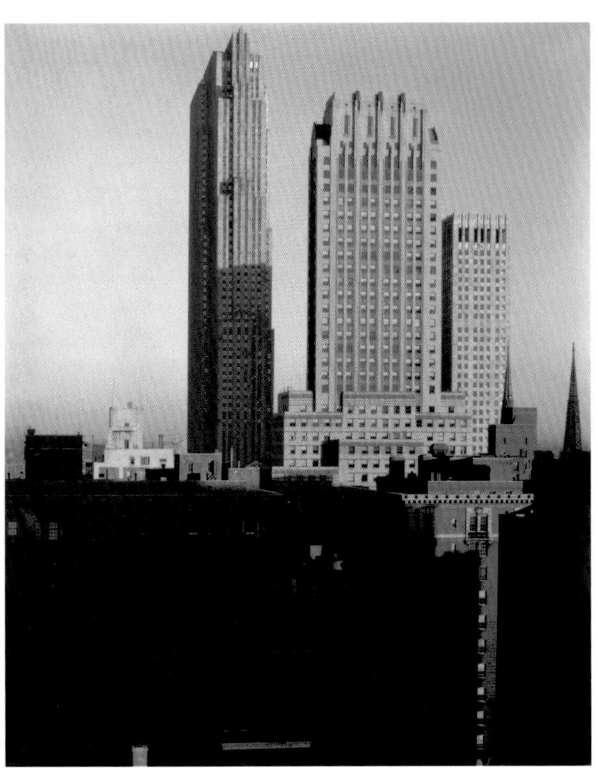

Alfred Stieglitz. *From the Shelton, West.* 1935

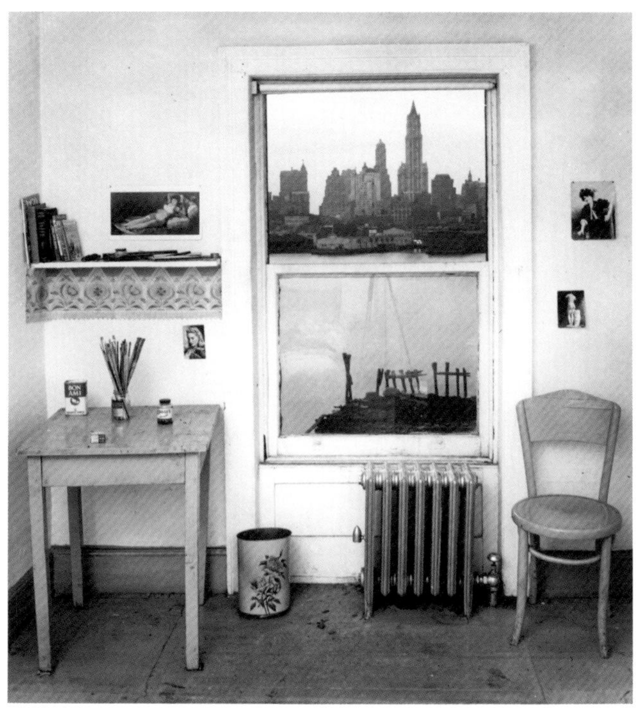

Rudy Burckhardt. *A View from Brooklyn I*. 1954

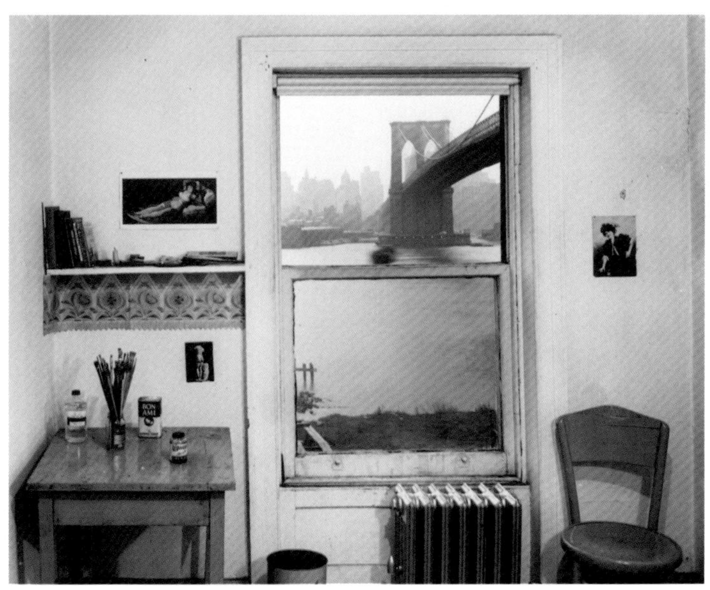

Rudy Burckhardt. *A View from Brooklyn II*. 1954

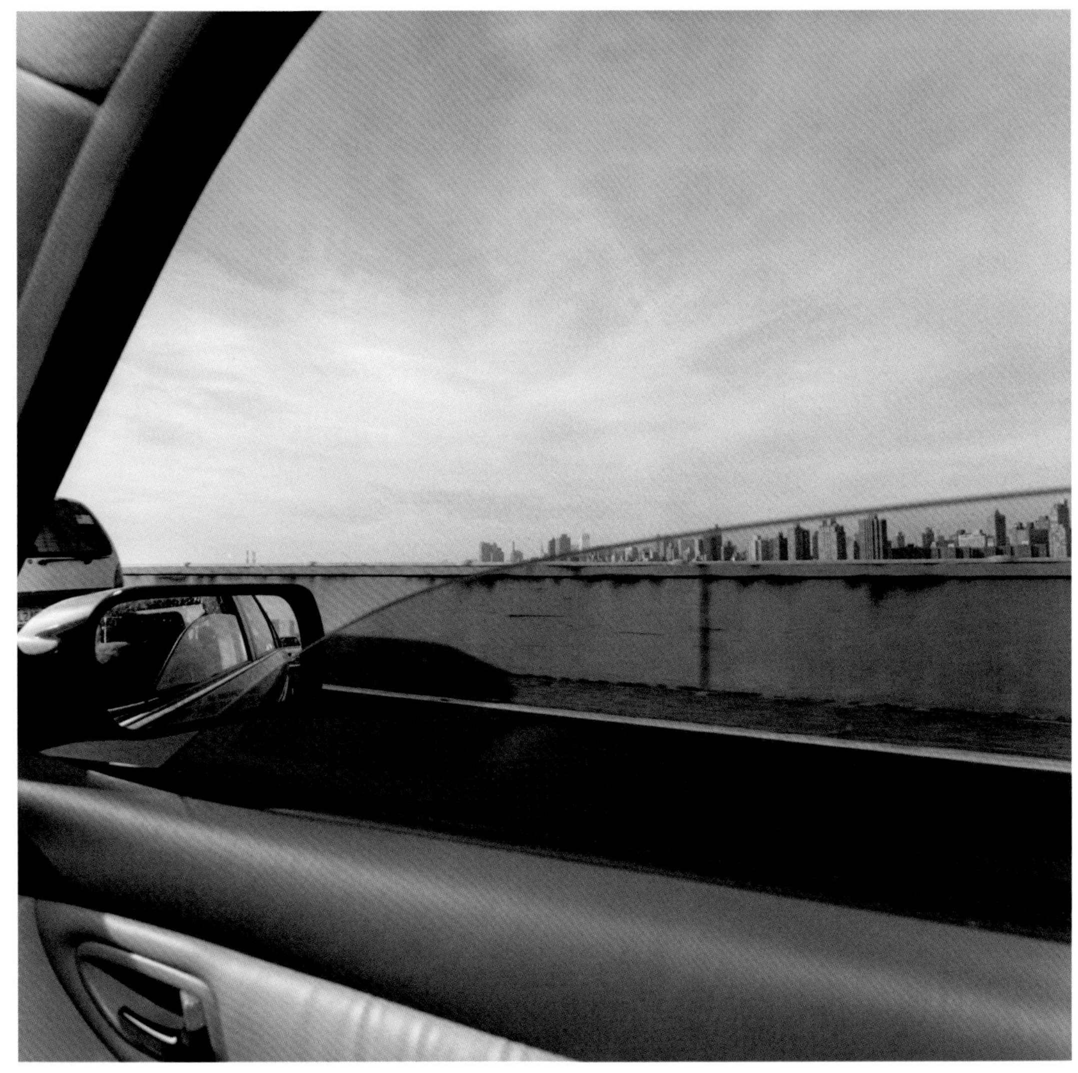

Lee Friedlander. *New York City*. 2002

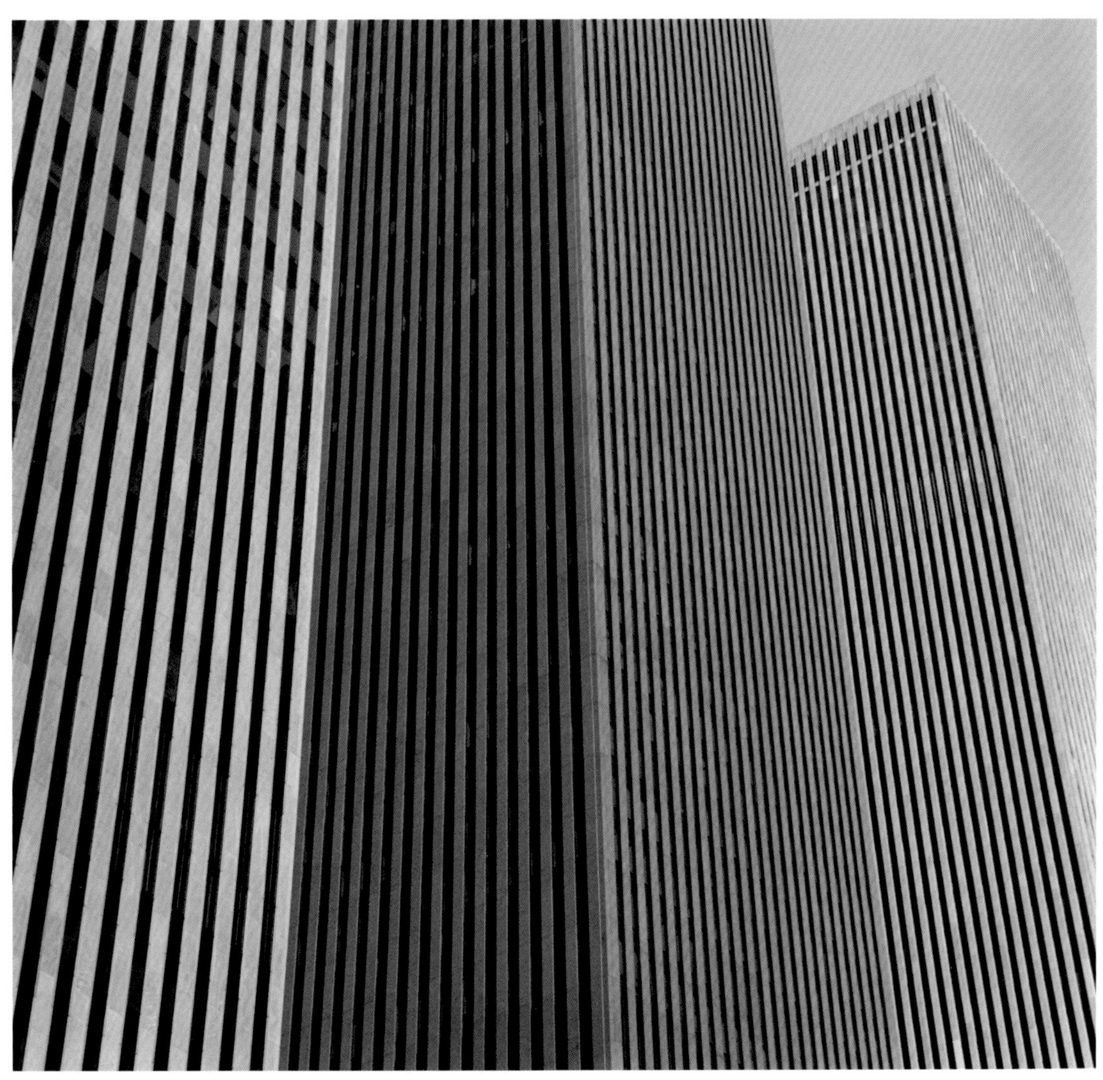

Harry Callahan. *New York*. 1974

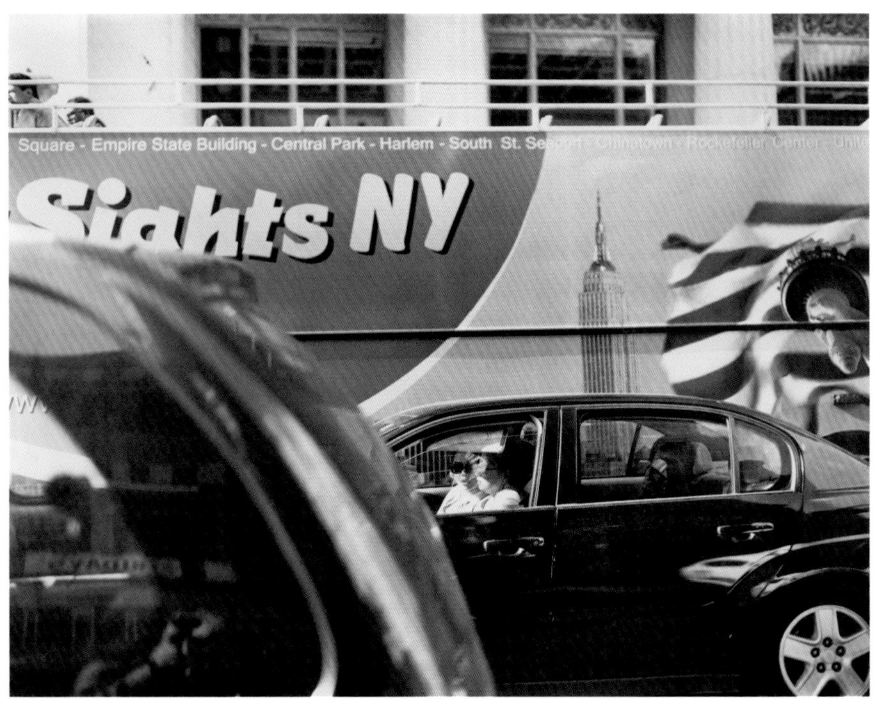

Michael Spano. *New York Sights*. 2005

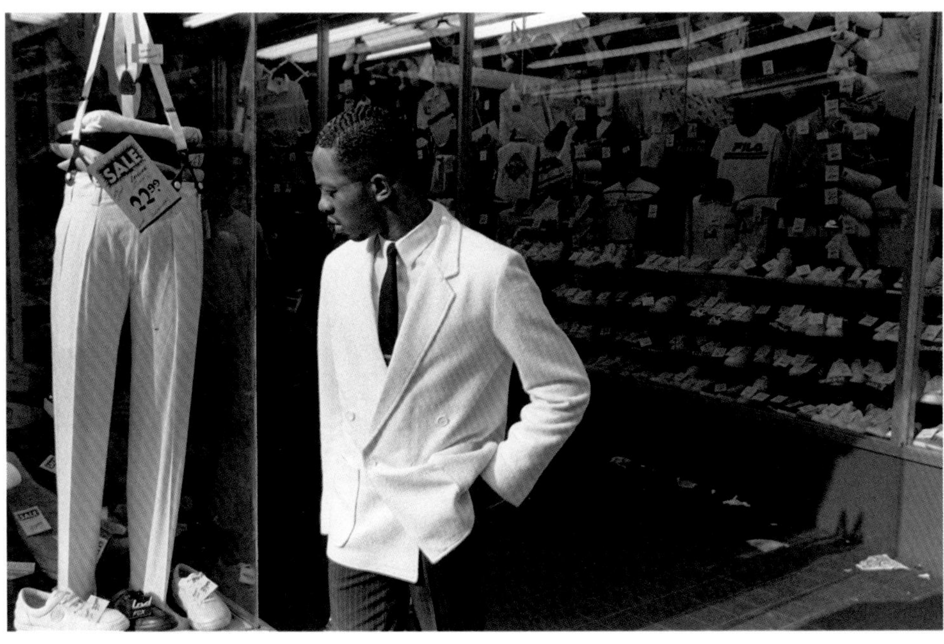

Dawoud Bey. *A Man Looking at Pants on Fulton Street*. 1989

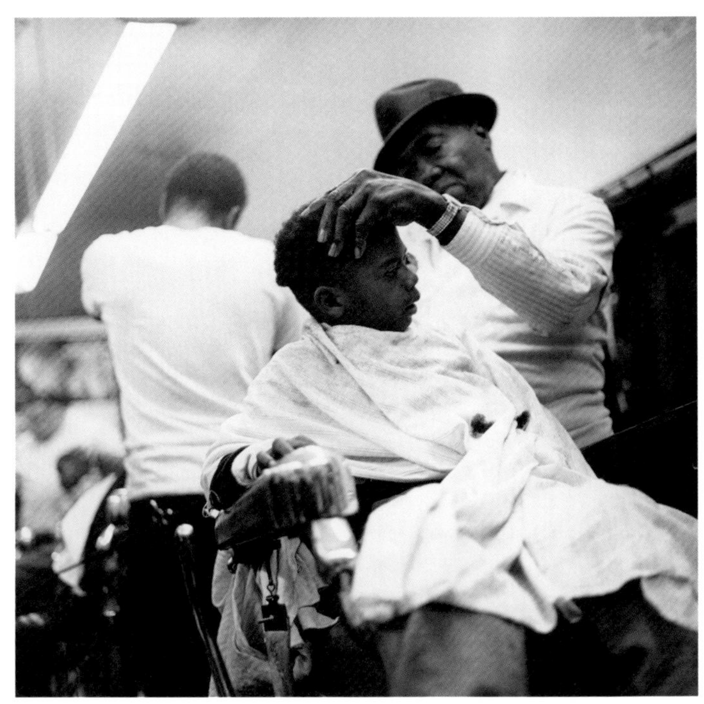

Jeffrey Scales. *Mr. Ben's Hand*. 1987

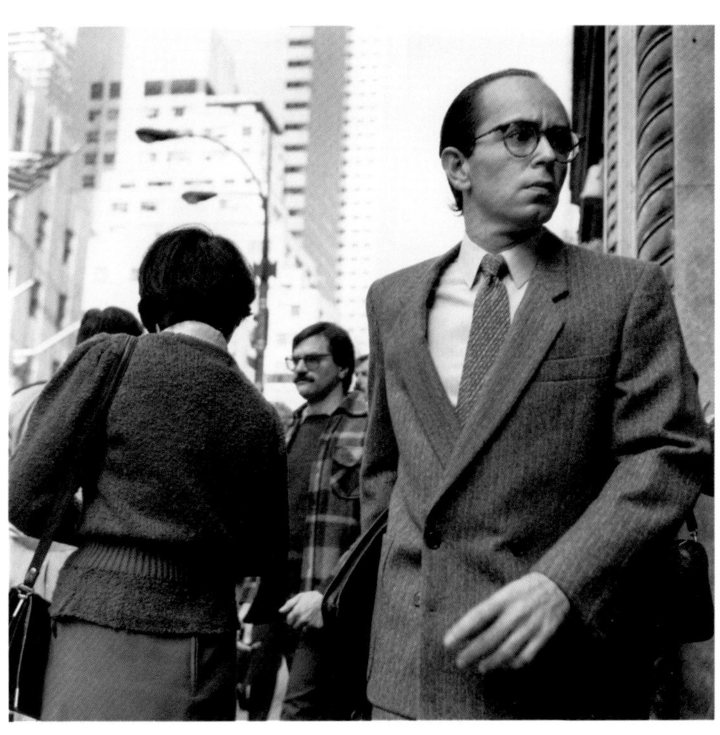

Roy Colmer. *Man by Saks Fifth Avenue*. 1985

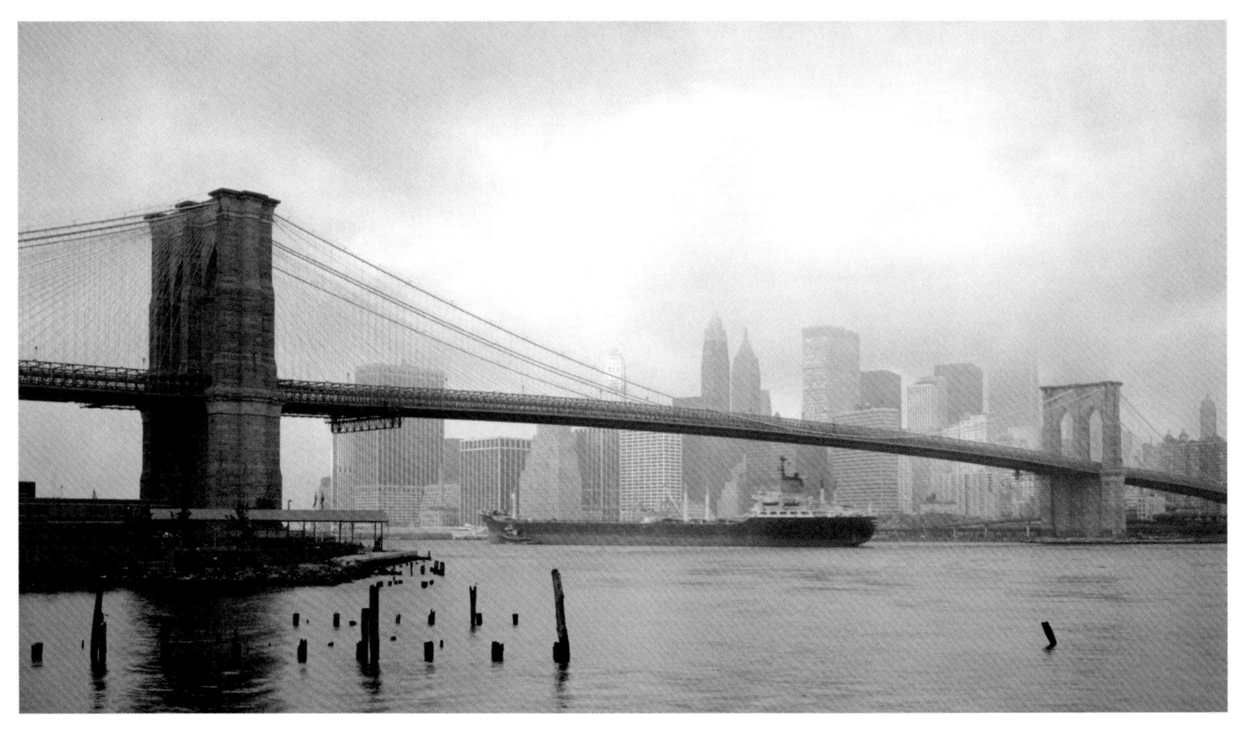

Richard Benson. *Brooklyn Bridge*. 1980

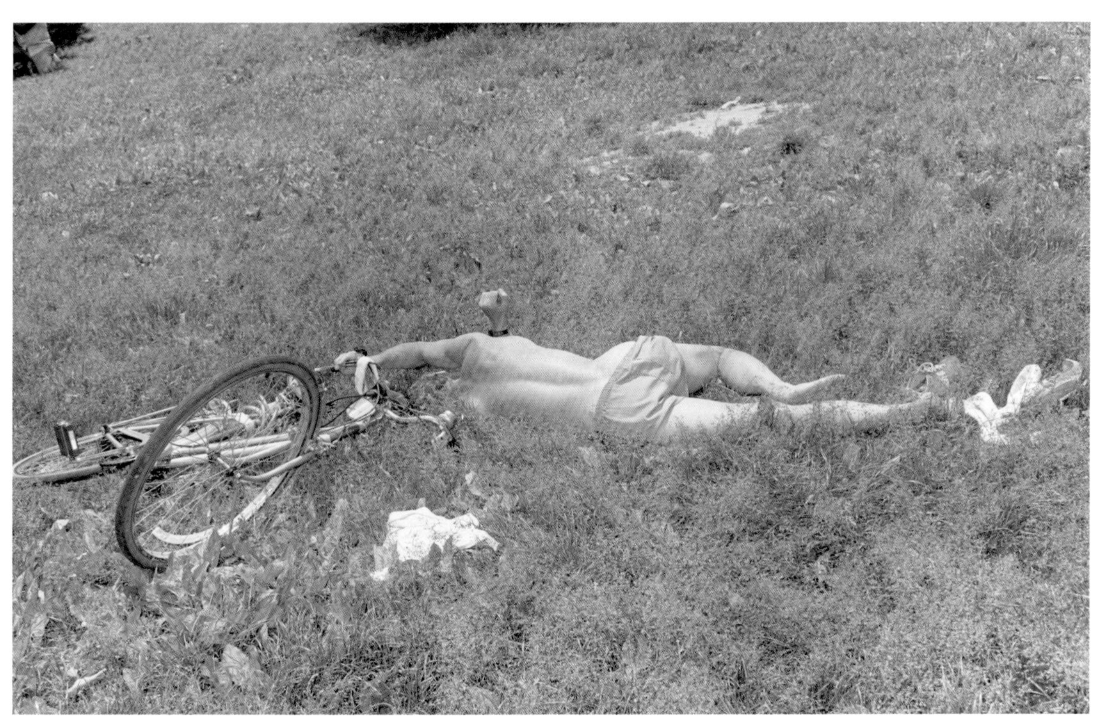

Tod Papageorge. *Central Park*. 1980

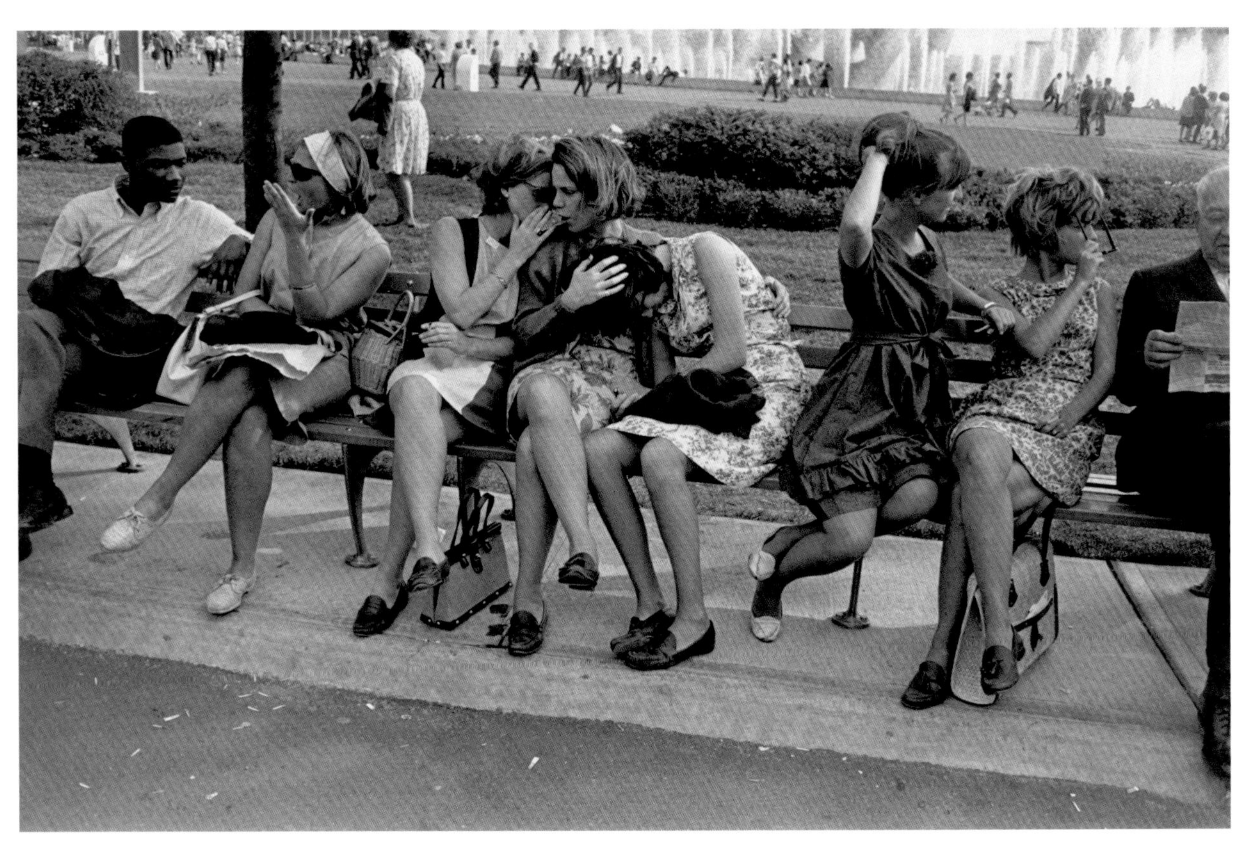

Garry Winogrand. *World's Fair, New York*. 1964

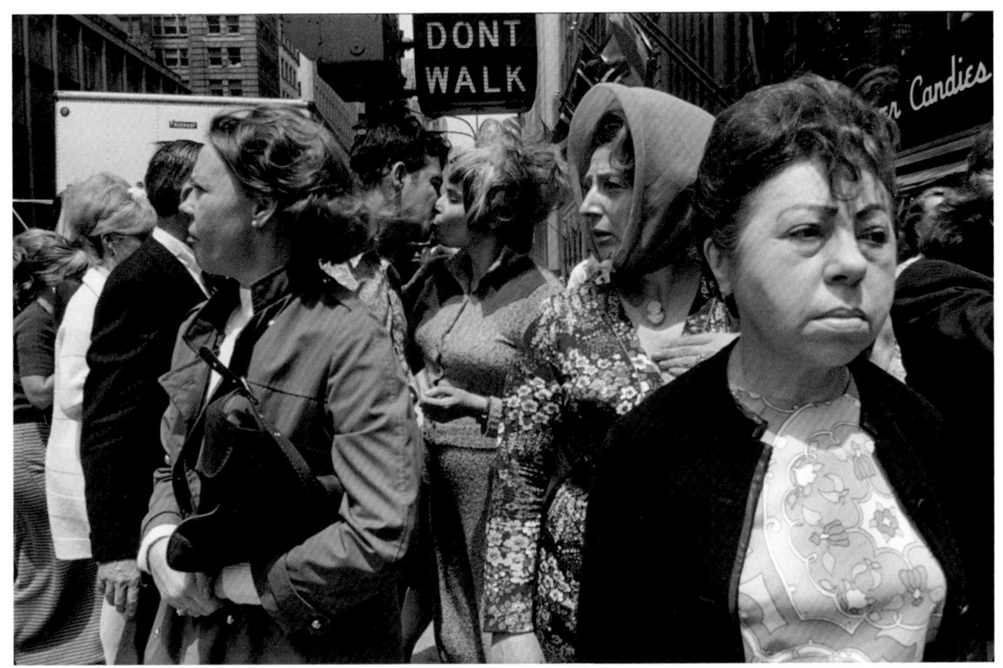

Tod Papageorge. *Fifth Avenue*. 1970

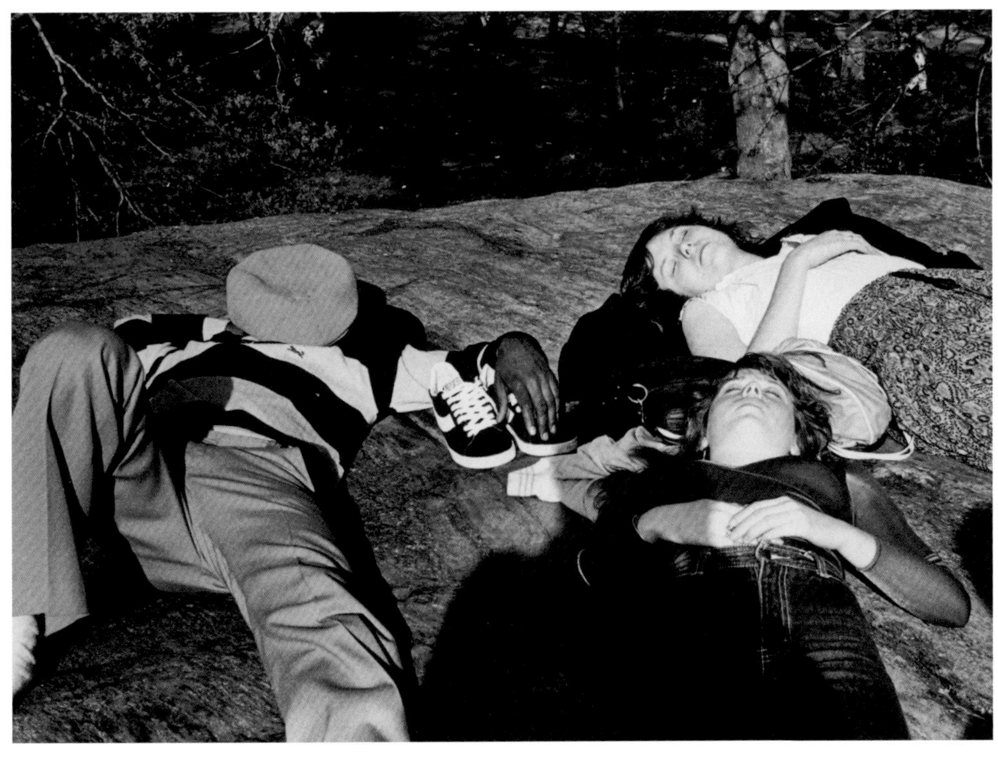

Beuford Smith. *Two Sun Bathers*. 1983

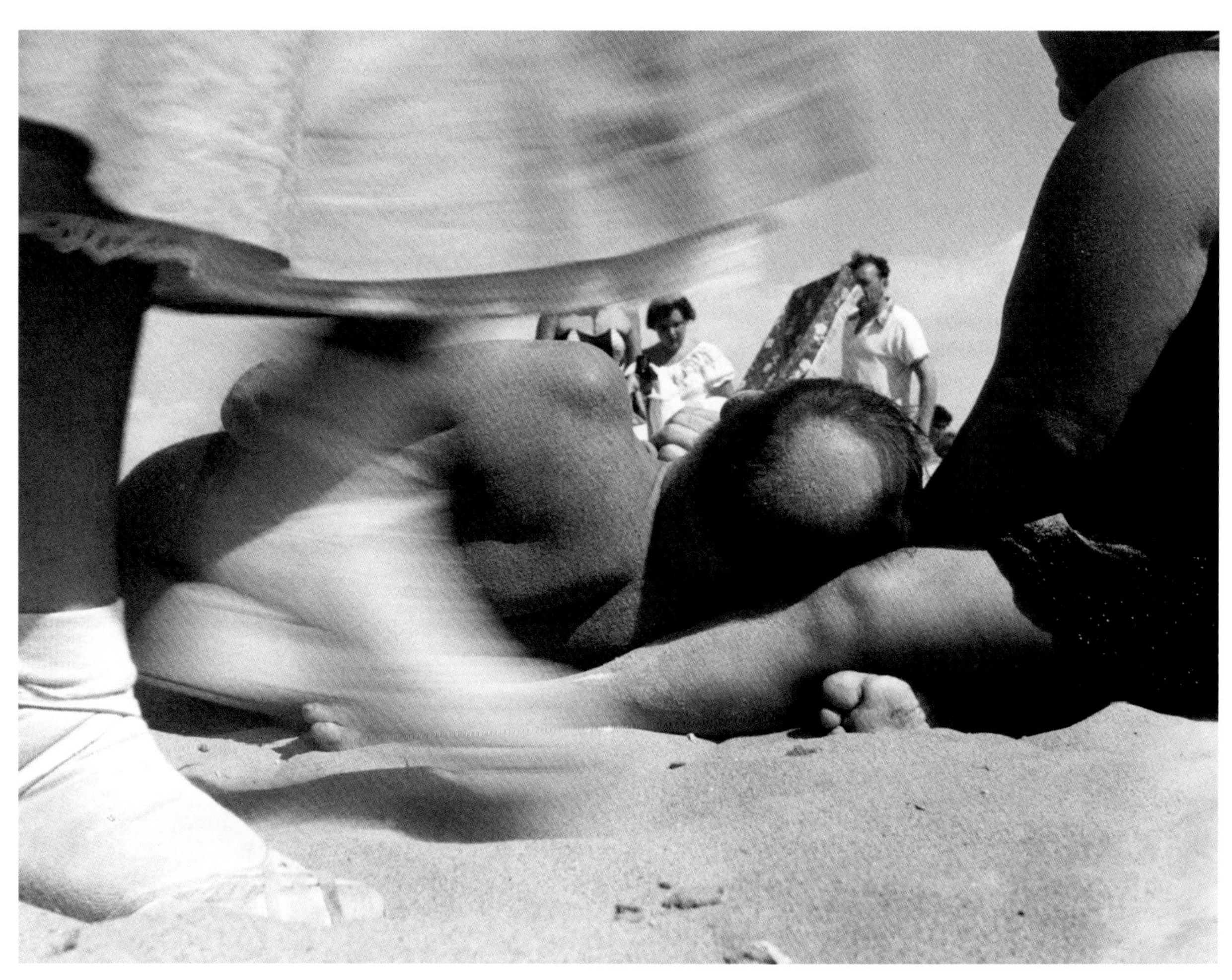

Leon Levinstein. *Coney Island*. 1952

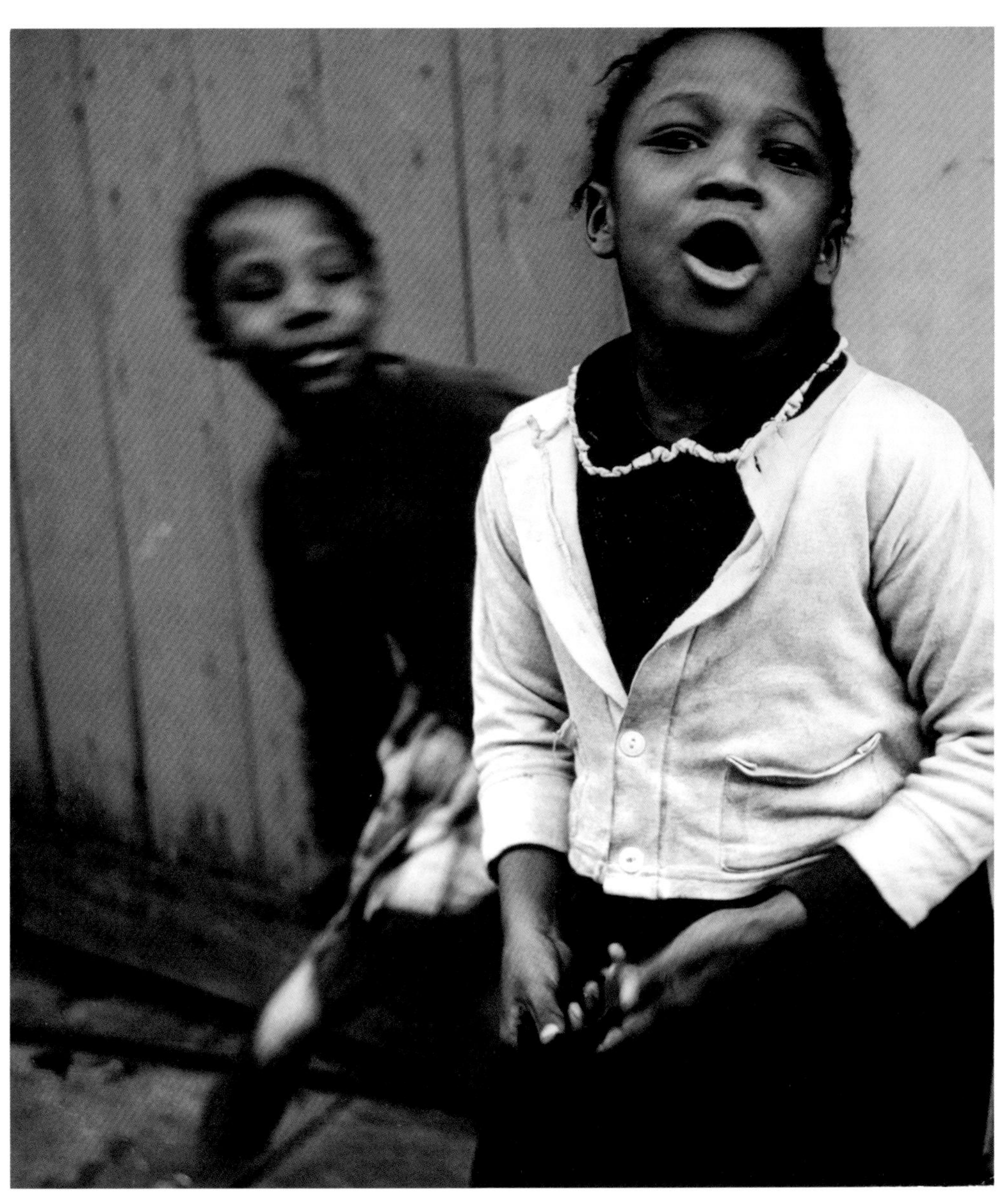

Vivian Cherry. *Harlem, New York City*. 1952

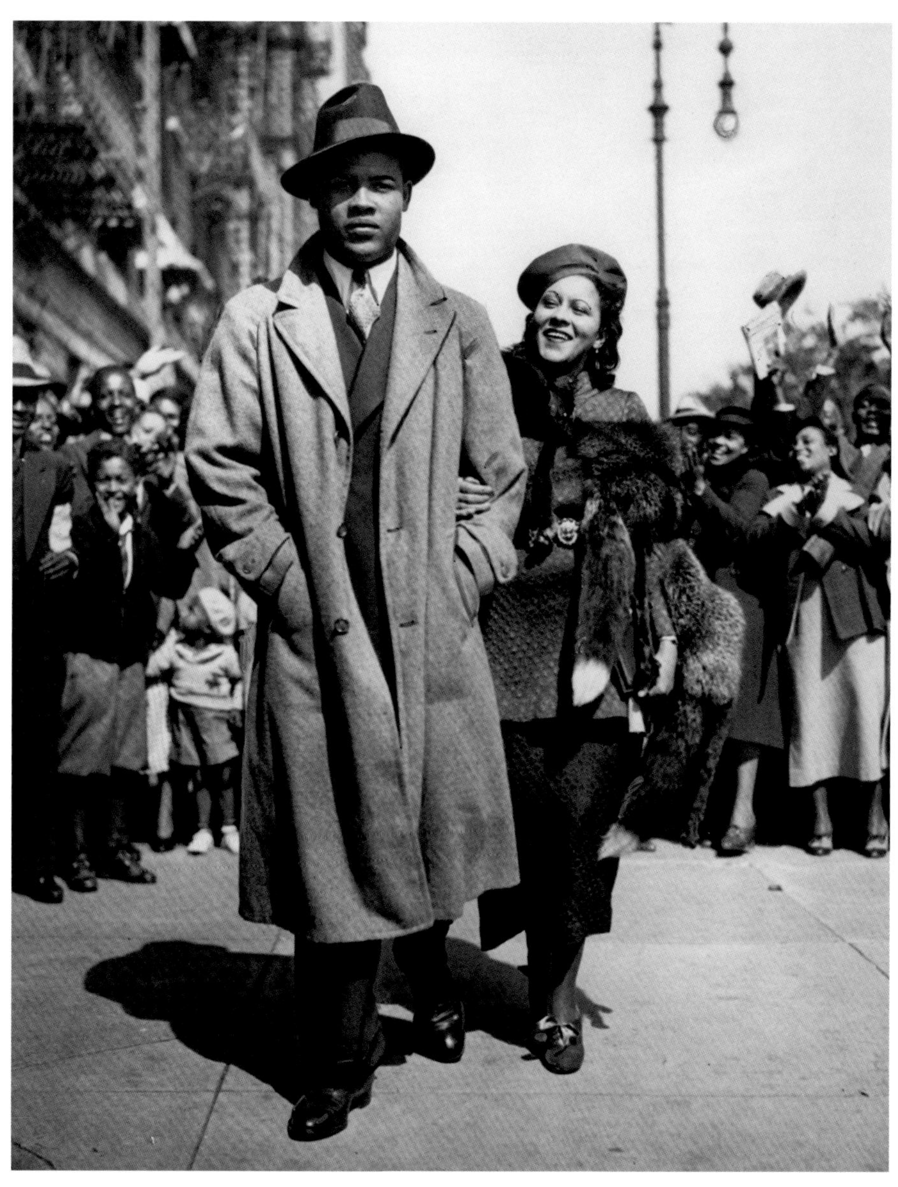

Times Wide World Photos. *Mr. and Mrs. Joe Louis Out for a Stroll.*
September 25, 1935

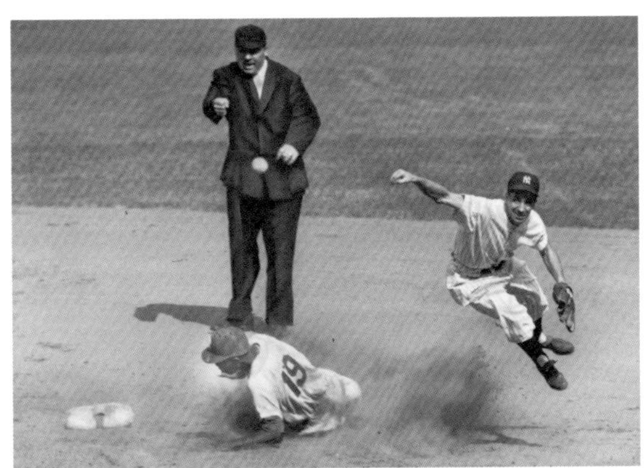

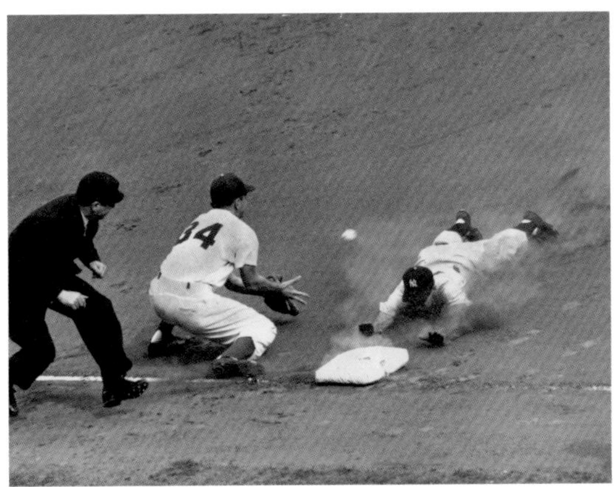

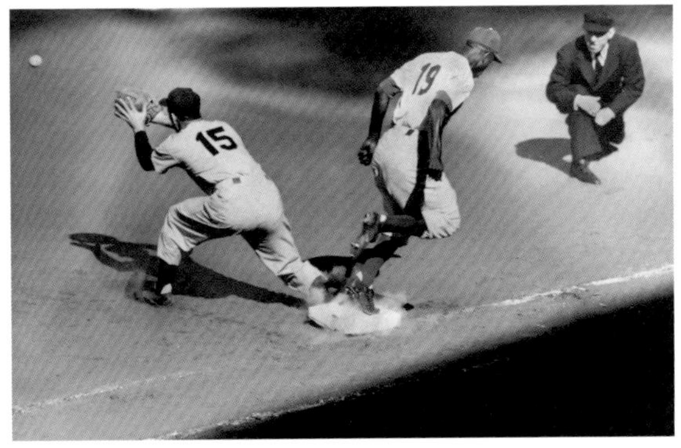

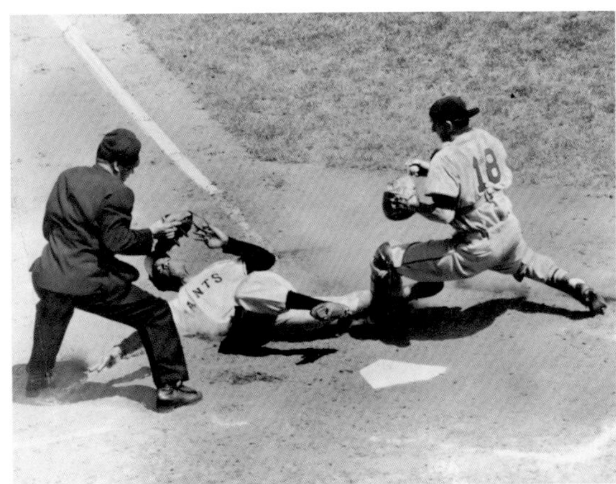

Right: Ernie Sisto. *World Series: Yankees vs. Dodgers (Gilliam Safe at First)*. October 2, 1953
Top: Ernie Sisto. *World Series: Yankees vs. Dodgers (Gilliam Slides into Second)*. September 28, 1955
Left: Pat Burns. *World Series: Yankees vs. Dodgers (Rizzuto Slides into Third)*. October 8, 1949
Bottom: Ernie Sisto. *Willie Mays Scoring on a Close Play at the Plate in Polo Grounds*. May 2, 1952

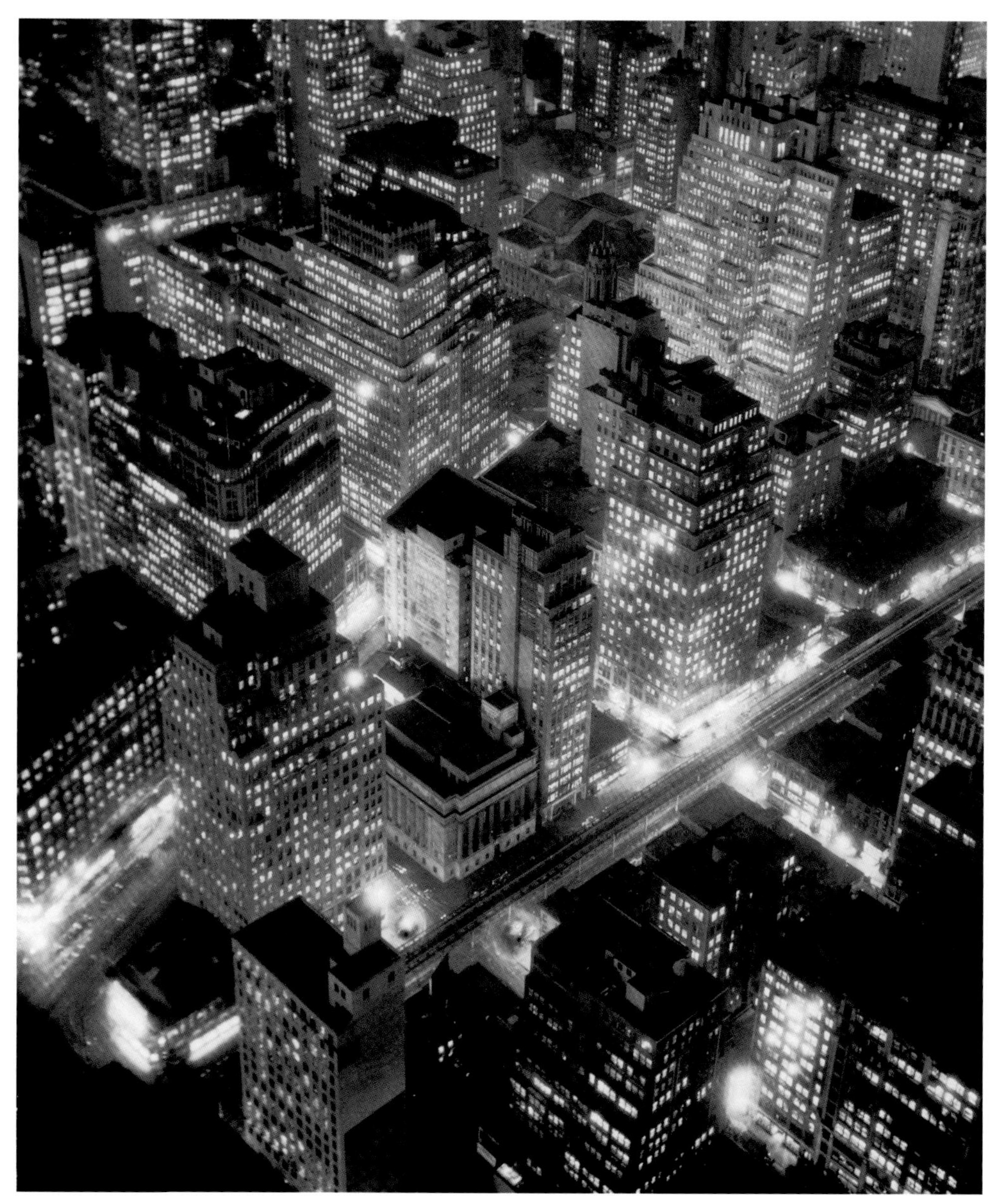

Berenice Abbott. *New York at Night*. 1932

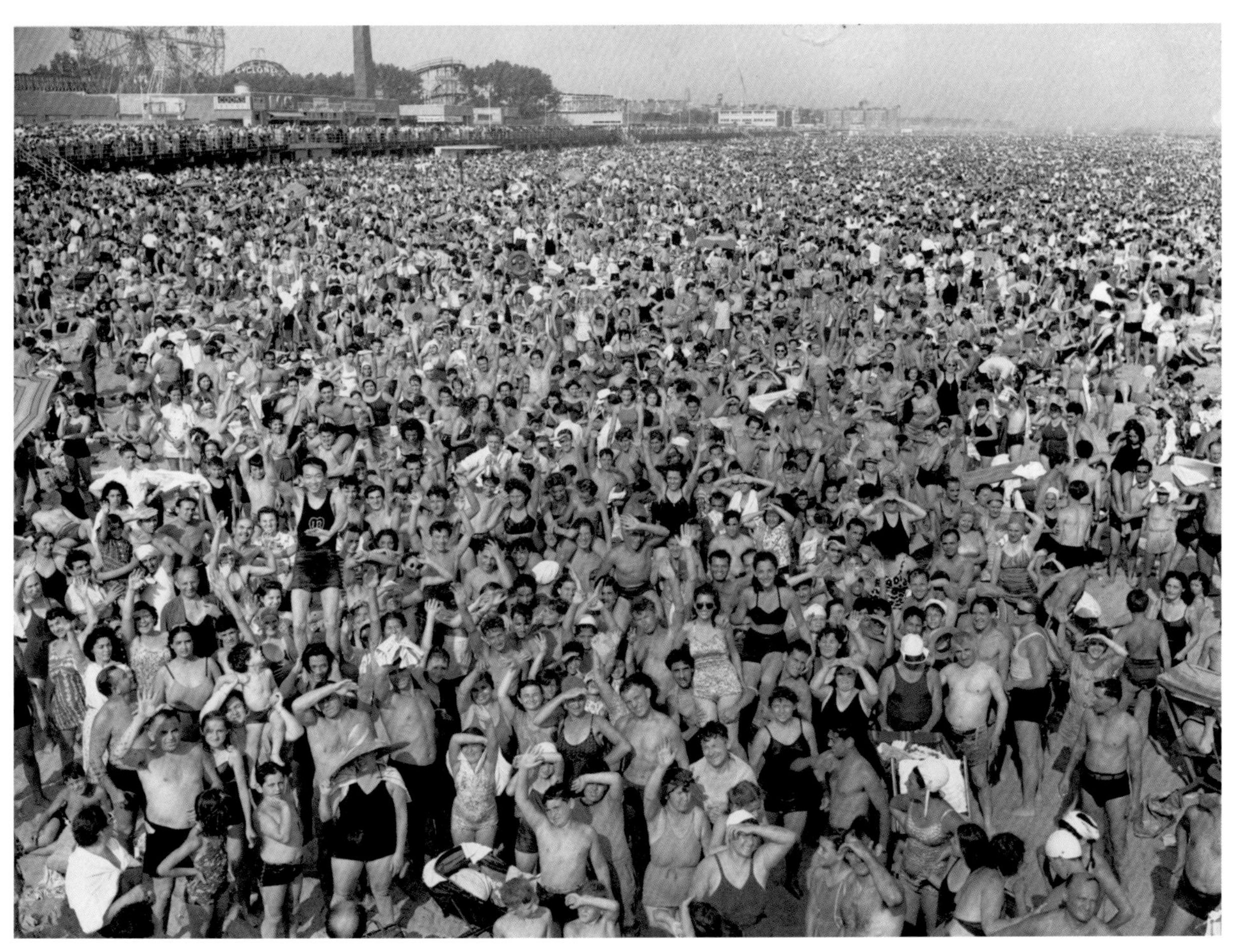

Weegee. *Coney Island*. c. 1939

checklist

All works are in the collection of The Museum of Modern Art and are gelatin silver prints unless otherwise indicated. In the dimensions, height precedes width. The number of the page on which the work appears is noted at the end of each entry.

Berenice Abbott. American, 1898–1991.
New York at Night. 1932. 12 7/8 x 10 9/16" (32.7 x 26.8 cm). Purchase [page 60]

Zito's Bakery, Bleecker Street. c. 1948. 9 1/2 x 7 1/2" (24.1 x 19.1 cm). Anonymous gift [page 9]

Diane Arbus. American, 1923–1971.
Woman with a Veil on Fifth Avenue, New York City. 1968. Printed by Neil Selkirk, 14 15/16 x 15 1/16" (37.9 x 38.3 cm). Purchase [page 35]

Anthony Barboza. American, born 1944.
Lionel Hampton, Village Gate. 1987. 22 1/4 x 15" (56.5 x 38.1 cm). Geraldine J. Murphy Fund [page 20]

Richard Benson. American, born 1943.
Brooklyn Bridge. 1980. Platinum/palladium print, 10 1/8 x 17 3/16" (25.7 x 43.7 cm). The Family of Man Fund [page 52]

Dawoud Bey. American, born 1953.
A Man Looking at Pants on Fulton Street. 1989. 15 7/8 x 23 3/8" (40.3 x 59.4 cm). E. T. Harmax Foundation Fund [page 50]

Margaret Bourke-White. American, 1904–1971.
Ornamental Gargoyle, Chrysler Building. 1934. 12 x 8 3/8" (30.5 x 21.3 cm). Gift of the photographer [page 40]

Rudy Burckhardt. American, born Switzerland. 1914–1999.
A View from Brooklyn I. 1954. Printed 1993, 10 5/16 x 9 3/16" (26.2 x 23.3 cm). Gift of CameraWorks, Inc., and purchase [page 47]

A View from Brooklyn II. 1954. Printed 1993, 8 15/16 x 10 5/8" (22.7 x 27 cm). Gift of CameraWorks, Inc., and purchase [page 47]

Pat Burns/The New York Times. American, 1909–1973.
World Series: Yankees vs. Dodgers (Rizzuto Slides into Third). October 8, 1949. 6 3/4 x 8 1/2" (17.2 x 21.6 cm). The New York Times Collection [page 59]

Harry Callahan. American, 1912–1999.
New York. 1974. 9 7/8 x 10" (25.1 x 25.4 cm). Gift of the photographer [page 49]

Henri Cartier-Bresson. French, 1908–2004.
An Eye at The Museum of Modern Art, New York. 1947. 13 5/8 x 9 1/8" (34.6 x 23.2 cm). Gift of Monroe Wheeler [page 15]

Near the Hall of Records, New York. 1947. Printed 1968, 15 5/16 x 22 13/16" (39 x 57.9 cm). Gift of the photographer [page 12]

Vivian Cherry. American, born 1920.
Harlem, New York City. 1952. 12 3/16 x 10 1/4" (31 x 26 cm). The Family of Man Fund [page 57]

Roy Colmer. British, born 1935.
Man by Saks Fifth Avenue. 1985. 15 x 15" (38.1 x 38.1 cm). Robert and Joyce Menschel Fund [page 51]

Lois Conner. American, born 1951.
Queens, New York. 1990. Platinum print, 6 1/2 x 16 1/2" (16.5 x 41.9 cm). Gift of the photographer [page 42]

Ted Croner. American, 1922–2005.
Taxi—New York—Night. 1947–48. 15 5/8 x 15 1/2" (39.7 x 39.4 cm). The Family of Man Fund [page 26]

Roy DeCarava. American, 1919–2009.
Child Playing at Curb, Eighth Avenue. 1952. 8 9/16 x 13 1/2" (21.7 x 34.3 cm). John Parkinson III Fund [page 38]

Walker Evans. American, 1903–1975.
Girl in Fulton Street, New York. 1929. 7 1/2 x 4 5/8" (19.1 x 11.8 cm). Gift of the photographer [page 34]

Louis Faurer. American, 1916–2001.
New York. 1950. 8 1/2 x 12 7/8" (21.6 x 32.7 cm). John Parkinson III Fund [page 23]

Ed Feingersh. American, 1925–1961.
Dance Hall, New York. c. 1953. 7 3/4 x 11 7/8" (19.7 x 30.2 cm). Gift of the photographer [page 23]

Larry Fink. American, born 1941.
Studio 54, New York City. May 1977. 14 1/16 x 13 7/8" (35.7 x 35.2 cm). Gift of the photographer [page 33]

Lee Friedlander. American, born 1934.
New York City. 1966. 5 3/4 x 8 11/16" (14.6 x 22.1 cm). Carl Jacobs Fund [page 13]

New York City. 1980. 18 5/8 x 12 3/8" (47.3 x 31.4 cm). The Family of Man Fund [page 37]

New York City. 2002. 14 15/16 x 14 3/4" (37.9 x 37.5 cm). Gift of the photographer [page 48]

Carl T. Gosset, Jr./The New York Times. American, 1924–1985.
Beatlemaniacs on the Loose. August 28, 1964. 7 3/8 x 10 1/8" (18.7 x 25.7 cm). The New York Times Collection [page 19]

Jan Groover. American, born 1943.
Untitled. 1981. Platinum/palladium print, 7 5/8 x 9 1/2" (19.4 x 24.1 cm). Anonymous extended loan and promised gift [page 43]

Lewis W. Hine. American, 1874–1940.
Italian Family Looking for Lost Baggage, Ellis Island, New York. 1905. Printed 1942, 5 9/16 x 4 5/16" (14.1 x 11 cm). Purchase [page 30]

Leon Levinstein. American, 1910–1988.
Coney Island. 1952. 9 3/4 x 12 5/16" (24.8 x 31.3 cm). Gift of the photographer [page 56]

Helen Levitt. American, 1913–2009.
New York. c. 1940. 8 7/8 x 13 1/4" (22.5 x 33.7 cm). Gift of the photographer [page 29]

New York. c. 1945. Printed c. 1981, 10 1/4 x 7 15/16" (26.2 x 20.2 cm). Gift of William H. Levitt [page 36]

Lisette Model. American, born Austria. 1901–1983.
Times Square. 1940. 15 9/16 x 9 9/16" (39.6 x 49.7 cm). Gift of the photographer [page 22]

Abelardo Morell. American, born Cuba 1948.
Camera Obscura Image of the Empire State Building in Bedroom. 1994. 17 15/16 x 22 1/2" (45.6 x 57.2 cm). Gift of the photographer in memory of Bill Beckler [page 16]

Barbara Morgan. American, 1900–1992.
Spring on Madison Square. 1938. 10 5/8 x 13 5/8" (27 x 34.6 cm). Purchase [page 17]

Tod Papageorge. American, born 1940.
Fifth Avenue. 1970. 7 3/4 x 11 11/16" (19.7 x 29.7 cm). John Parkinson III Fund [page 55]

Central Park. 1980. 10 1/4 x 15 5/8" (26 x 39.7 cm). Acquired with matching funds from Samuel William Sax and the National Endowment for the Arts [page 53]

Gordon Parks. American, 1912–2006.
From the photostory "The Atmosphere of Crime," *Life* magazine. September 9, 1957. 12 3/8 x 17 7/16" (31.4 x 44.3 cm). Gift of the photographer in honor of Edward Steichen [page 27]

Irving Penn. American, 1917–2009.
Ballet Theatre, New York. 1947. 13 3/4 x 19 1/4" (34.9 x 48.9 cm). Gift of the photographer [page 45]

Thomas Roma. American, born 1950.
Untitled from the series *Come Sunday*. 1991–94. 14 x 18 5/8" (35.6 x 47.3 cm). Gift of the photographer [page 31]

Jeffrey Scales. American, born 1954.
Mr. Ben's Hand. 1987. 19 1/4 x 19 3/16" (48.9 x 48.7 cm). E. T. Harmax Foundation Fund [page 51]

Cindy Sherman. American, born 1954.
Untitled Film Still #21. 1978. 7 1/2 x 9 1/2" (19.1 x 24.1 cm). Horace W. Goldsmith Fund through Robert B. Menschel [page 13]

Untitled Film Still #54. 1980. 6 13/16 x 9 7/16" (17.3 x 24 cm). Acquired through the generosity of Peter Norton [page 24]

Ernie Sisto/The New York Times. American, 1904–1989.
Willie Mays Scoring on a Close Play at the Plate in Polo Grounds. May 2, 1952. 7 x 8 1/2" (17.8 x 21.6 cm). The New York Times Collection [page 59]

World Series: Yankees vs. Dodgers (Gilliam Safe at First). October 2, 1953. 8 5/8 x 13" (22 x 33 cm). The New York Times Collection [page 59]

World Series: Yankees vs. Dodgers (Gilliam Slides into Second). September 28, 1955. 8 13/16 x 12 3/16" (22.4 x 31 cm). The New York Times Collection [page 59]

Beuford Smith. American, born 1941.
Two Sun Bathers. 1983. 9 15/16 x 13 3/16" (25.2 x 33.5 cm). E. T. Harmax Foundation Fund [page 55]

Michael Spano. American, born 1949.
New York Sights. 2005. 27 3/4 x 34 7/8" (70.5 x 88.6 cm). Lois and Bruce Zenkel Fund [page 50]

Edward Steichen. American, born Luxembourg. 1879–1973.
The Maypole. 1932. 13 1/4 x 10 7/16" (33.7 x 26.5 cm). Gift of the photographer [page 14]

Alfred Stieglitz. American, 1864–1946.
City of Ambition. 1910. Photogravure, 13 3/8 x 10 1/4" (34 x 26 cm). Purchase [page 41]

From the Shelton, West. 1935. 9 1/2 x 7 1/2" (24.1 x 19.1 cm). The Alfred Stieglitz Collection. Gift of Miss Georgia O'Keeffe [page 46]

From the Shelton, West. 1935. 9 5/8 x 7 1/2" (24.5 x 19.1 cm). The Alfred Stieglitz Collection. Gift of Miss Georgia O'Keeffe [page 46]

Paul Strand. American, 1890–1976.
Fifth Avenue, New York. 1915. Platinum print, 12 1/4 x 8 3/16" (31.1 x 20.8 cm). Gift of the photographer [page 39]

Thomas Struth. German, born 1954.
Sixth Avenue at 50th Street, New York/ Midtown. 1978. Printed 1993, 16 5/16 x 22 5/8" (41.4 x 57.5 cm). The Family of Man Fund [page 11]

Madoka Takagi. Japanese, born 1956.
North View from Municipal Building. 1991. Platinum print, 7 1/2 x 9 9/16" (19.1 x 24.3 cm). Horace W. Goldsmith Fund through Robert B. Menschel [page 43]

Times Wide World Photos.
Mr. and Mrs. Joe Louis Out for a Stroll. September 25, 1935. 8 3/4 x 6 5/8" (22.2 x 16.8 cm). The New York Times Collection [page 58]

The Mayor and a Baby Exchange Smiles. December 8, 1938. 9 3/8 x 7 3/4" (23.9 x 19.7 cm). The New York Times Collection [page 28]

Underwood and Underwood.
Above Fifth Avenue, Looking North. 1905. 9 1/2 x 7 5/16" (24.1 x 18.6 cm). The New York Times Collection [page 10]

James Van Der Zee. American, 1886–1983.
Unity Athletic and Social Club, Inc. 1926. 7 7/8 x 10 1/16" (20 x 25.5 cm). Samuel J. Wagstaff, Jr., Fund [page 44]

Weegee (Arthur Fellig). American, born Austria. 1899–1968.
Coney Island. c. 1939. 10 5/16 x 13 11/16" (26.2 x 34.8 cm). Anonymous gift [page 61]

Macy's Thanksgiving Day Parade. c. 1942. 10 9/16 x 13 5/16" (26.8 x 33.8 cm). The Family of Man Fund [page 25]

Dan Weiner. American, 1919–1959.
New Year's Eve, Times Square. 1951. 9 1/4 x 13 3/16" (23.5 x 33.5 cm). Gift of Sandra Weiner [page 21]

Garry Winogrand. American, 1928–1984.
El Morocco. 1955. 9 1/16 x 13 3/8" (23 x 34 cm). Purchase and gift of Barbara Schwartz in memory of Eugene M. Schwartz [page 32]

World's Fair, New York. 1964. Printed 1974, 8 9/16 x 12 15/16" (21.7 x 32.9 cm). Gift of N. Carol Lipis [page 54]

Metropolitan Museum of Art Centennial Ball, New York. 1969. Printed 1974, 8 9/16 x 12 13/16" (21.7 x 32.5 cm). Gift of N. Carol Lipis [page 32]

Muhammad Ali–Oscar Bonavena Press Conference, New York. 1970. 10 5/8 x 15 15/16" (27 x 40.5 cm). Purchase [page 18]

George Zimbel. Canadian, born 1929.
Jacqueline and John Kennedy, New York City. 1960. Printed 1990, 11 1/8 x 16 5/8" (28.3 x 42.2 cm). The Family of Man Fund [page 19]